THE BEAT GOES ON

PERSPECTIVES ON THE NEWS

Other works in the series:

The New News v. The Old News:
The Press and Politics in the 1990s
Essays by Jay Rosen and Paul Taylor

Covering the World:
International Television News Services
Essay by Lewis A. Friedland

Reinventing the Newspaper
Essays by Frank Denton and Howard Kurtz

At What Price?
Libel Law and Freedom of the Press
Essays by Martin London and Barbara Dill

PERSPECTIVES
ON THE NEWS

Tom Rosenstiel

THE BEAT GOES ON

President Clinton's First Year with the Media

A Twentieth Century Fund Essay

The Twentieth Century Fund sponsors and supervises timely analyses of economic policy, foreign affairs, and domestic political issues. Not-for-profit and nonpartisan, the Fund was founded in 1919 and endowed by Edward A. Filene.

Library of Congress Cataloging-in-Publication Data

Rosenstiel, Tom.
  The beat goes on : President Clinton's first year with the media : essay / by Tom Rosenstiel.
    p. cm. (Perspectives on the news series)
  Includes index.
  ISBN 0-87078-369-6 : $9.95
  1. Clinton, Bill. 1946– —Relations with journalists. 2. Press and politics—United States—History—20th century. 3. United States—Politics and government—1993– I. Twentieth Century Fund. II. Title.
E886.2.R67   1994
973.929'092—dc20

94–25761
CIP

Cover Design: Claude Goodwin
Manufactured in the United States of America.

FOREWORD

I n a democracy, the information the public actually receives serves as the context in which judgments are formed, voting patterns are shaped, and, ultimately, policy choices are made. For several decades, the Twentieth Century Fund has sponsored research and writing about the interaction of media and politics. In 1992, for example, we convened a group of journalists, editors, producers, and their critics as a task force on television coverage of the presidential election. After several meetings, they issued a report, entitled *1-800-PRESIDENT*, which offered a series of suggested improvements to the news industry. We already have started preliminary meetings with a similar group focused on the 1996 campaign and related issues.

We also currently support a continuing series of publications, Perspectives on the News, that explores American media, broadly conceived, including changes in the competitive environment, technology, and journalistic standards. Each part of the series also discusses the implications of changes in the media for coverage of politics and public policy. Previous volumes include *The New News v. The Old News* with essays by Jay Rosen and Paul Taylor, *Reinventing the Newspaper* with essays by Frank Denton and Howard Kurtz, *At What Price?* with essays by Martin London and Barbara Dill, and *Covering the World* by Lewis A. Friedland.

In this essay, Tom Rosenstiel focuses on an area that merits exceptional attention: the relationship between the American president and the press corps that covers him. The author, Washington media and political correspondent for the *Los Angeles Times*, specifically addresses that relationship during the first year of the Clinton presidency.

The Beat Goes On: President Clinton's First Year with the Media is not Tom Rosenstiel's first in-depth analysis of how the press chooses and presents information. His earlier book, *Strange Bedfellows: How Television and the Presidential Candidates Changed American Politics, 1992*, was an insightful exploration of forces whose impact we see on the screen every day but that rarely are explained in depth. In this work, he extends his previous research and analysis by asking whether lessons have been learned from what many believe was a groundbreaking portrayal by the media of the 1992 presidential campaign.

Even though self-conscious analysis by the press of its actions has increased apace in recent years, the open discussion of coverage of the 1992 campaign—and the extent to which the public seemed part of the reexamination—was extraordinary. In retrospect, the 1988 campaign was exceptional for the degree to which press coverage was successfully manipulated. In addition, that contest continued the process of ever more negative coverage of candidates and obsessive concentration on the "horse race" rather than the debate over issues. While 1992 started out, in many ways, in an equally disappointing fashion, a variety of factors led to what was perceived as an increase in direct candidate communication with the voters and sharp improvement in television's exploration of the substantive issues at stake.

In the pages that follow, Rosenstiel concludes that if lessons were learned in 1992, they were soon forgotten. He argues that when it comes to how the press covers the president, it is largely business as usual. And, while none of the players on either side is totally guilt-free, Rosenstiel does not spare his colleagues and the news outlets they represent. But Rosenstiel goes further, bravely venturing into controversy by offering specific and provocative suggestions for press reform. Even when one disagrees with his remedies, he retains our respect because of his candor and thoughtfulness. His concerns are part of what appears to be a growing awareness by many media professionals that there must be a better way.

The challenge, serious journalists recognize, is to provide an accurate depiction of events, a clear analysis of ideas, avoid manipulation by spin doctors, and still present information to the public in a way that lets it be the ultimate judge. Meeting this challenge is especially important in view of other developments in American society. Many have noted the decline of the power and influence of political parties and indeed of many other critical institutions of American life and civic culture. In this environment, it may be that a larger role has been thrust upon the press than it is capable of handling. After all, providing what Ben Bradlee, former editor of the

Washington Post, once called the "best available version of the truth" each day is not congruent with the totality of reasoned argument, civic education, and informed mediation between the public and candidates that should be at the heart of the democratic process. But whether they have sought their preeminent role or even are well suited to it, modern media are the selectors and providers of most of the information citizens actually have about their leaders and their government.

At a time when the press is disturbingly prone to psychoanalyze those in power, Rosenstiel notes a tendency in the media to pass instant judgments that are frequently revised, and to emphasize who's ahead over their ideas. It is fair to ask whether some of the matters that trouble us are the results of circumstances that have made journalists into celebrities, news shows into multimillion-dollar businesses, and caused many in the press to feel pressure from nontraditional media to sensationalize their coverage. Perhaps, too, the rapid evolution of American popular culture to include public discourse about matters that were formally relegated to gossip or protected by notions of privacy has merely swept the press along for the ride. Whatever the reasons, the idea that anything about an individual is fair game and that every move by a political figure should be treated with cynicism has contributed to souring the public about both politics and the press.

Democratic theory tells us that an informed and interested public is the key to successful self-governance. Thomas Jefferson is often quoted on the value of newspapers, but his ideal was a press that fulfilled the imperative of educating the public. As he put it, "If a nation expects to be ignorant and free . . . it expects what never was and never will be." In an era of increasingly complex choices and renewed impetus for the mechanisms of direct democracy, such as initiative, referendum, recall, and term limits, the overwhelming importance of a press that enlightens (even when that means forgoing titillation) is, if anything, more important than ever.

The government cannot change the way the press operates, and shouldn't try. Market forces play a powerful role, but today they are widely seen as part of the reason for the disturbing direction the media have taken. And, while no one can be completely sure what the public wants or needs, one can hope that journalists will always see their main responsibility as providing the information the public must have for self-government. On behalf of the Trustees of the Twentieth Century Fund, I want to thank Tom Rosenstiel for his efforts and his insight. It is some comfort to know that there are journalists who are as troubled by recent media trends as those outside the trade are—after all, the only real reform of the press must come from within the press.

Richard C. Leone, *President*
The Twentieth Century Fund
May 1994

CONTENTS

Foreword   by Richard C. Leone   v

Introduction   1

1/Campaign '92   4

2/Out with the Old   7

3/Using the New Media   14

4/Learning to Manage the Old Media   19

5/The Old Media React to the New   23

6/Return to Horse Race Coverage   26

7/The Era of Subjectivity   30

8/The New Media Have Lowered Journalistic Standards   35

9/Beyond 1994   43

Notes   50

Index   55

About the Author   59

INTRODUCTION

Americans love forgetting. In the culture of disposable diapers and "instant classics," the past is something to be let go, and "Today is the first day of the rest of your life." In politics, Bill Clinton, the first president born after World War II, talks about "reinventing government" and "making a new beginning" when he cuts the bureaucracy or introduces his annual budget.

So it is with the way America elects its leaders. Once the awful campaign season finally ends, why dwell on it? "Let's get these guys off the TV screen already," one voter from the oft-interviewed Macomb County, Michigan, told NBC in the fall of 1992. The media turn the day after election to the transition—the planning and appointments of the new administration. Washingtonians turn to trying to score tickets to the Inaugural. Call it political pragmatism, or simple good taste. The king is dead; long live the king.

This pragmatic futurism, however, tends to leave our recent political history to mythmakers and partisan revisionism, to overdrawn snap judgments by pundits and exhausted political writers. And it creates a bias toward detecting change where something less revolutionary and more complicated may have occurred. The presidential campaign of 1992 has been described as an event of epochal change in how American politics works—the end of the traditional media's control over the public dialogue, a radical shift in American attitudes toward social problems, toward economic policy, the Vietnam War, even sexual mores.

Certainly the 1992 campaign was a point of convergence. We saw the end of one administration and the beginning of another. We saw the rise of new forms of communication and challenges, in the form of Ross Perot, to the methods of the parties, the system of presidential primaries, and the Old Media that had evolved around them. The campaign

1

signaled a breakthrough in the use of some forms of technology and in
the ability of the public to shape the dialogue of the campaign. There
was certainly change. But where was this change leading us?

In this paper, I will attempt to look more closely, with the advan-
tage of a year and a half having passed since the election, at how the
relationship between television and political leadership has changed.
I will do so by providing a detailed analysis of how the Clinton administration has attempted to use the media to communicate its message and how the media have covered or communicated images of
Clinton to the public. I will explore whether what I will call the Old
Media are becoming obsolete, a filter increasingly to be bypassed by
political leaders. I will detail how the Old Media have changed since
the election, and what role the New Media have played. And I will
offer some thoughts on 1996 and how the press should change if it is
to better fulfill its obligations to the public and ensure its own economic survival.

To do so, this paper will rely on extensive interviews I have conducted with all the key members of the administration involved in
communications, dozens of members of the White House press corps,
and study of the network coverage of Clinton and Clinton's use of television technology. In brief, I will argue:

1.   The Clinton administration never had a conscious strategy to
      attempt to bypass the Old Media. But that impression was
      unwittingly created by the administration's inexperience and
      incompetent handling of the traditional White House press
      corps and by its interesting experiments in using technology
      and the New Media. The myth of bypass was furthered, too,
      by the fears of the White House press corps about their own
      relevance and by exaggerated press coverage of how much
      the public's use of the media had changed.

2.   Despite the fears of some journalists in the early days of the
      Clinton administration, the Old Media are not obsolete. The
      media spectrum has become wider, which has made each
      point on the spectrum less important. The *New York Times*
      and CBS have diminished in importance, but they are not
      irrelevant and cannot be bypassed. The New Media general-
      ly plays a supplemental role, but they can emerge as mo-
      mentarily dominant, depending on the situation. The key to

political communication now is understanding which media are right for which message and time, a task that makes employing the media to communicate one's political and governmental agenda more difficult, not easier as some have imagined.

3. The task of communication has also become more difficult because of changes in the Old Media. The traditional press did not continue in the mode in which it finished the campaign of 1992. Instead of continuing to move in the direction of becoming more policy oriented than before, the press has resumed the course of moving further away from objective reporting and becoming quicker to make judgments, interpret, and analyze. At the same time, the Old Media have allowed their journalistic standards to decline in the face of the New Media. Both of these changes are a mistake, and they are based on false choices the traditional news media are making about how to survive economically. The way for the press to thrive in the new media environment is not to begin to resemble its new competition, to move in the direction of "infotainment" and tabloid journalism. Rather, the press needs to distinguish itself from the new media by reaffirming its traditional and legitimate role. It must hold even more firmly to traditional journalistic standards and approach to content. It needs to be even more clear that, unlike its competition, it is engaged in public service and is committed to high standards of accuracy and proof. It must demonstrate that its purpose is to provide people with information they need to live their lives. Though this may seem difficult in the short run, over the long term I believe this is the only way the press can play to its strengths and guarantee its future.

4. In 1996, the New Media will become more important again than they have been during the administration, as voters and politicians temporarily seek a more direct relationship with one another. The press in the campaign should see itself as playing the role more of referee or firefighter over the political dialogue and should orient itself away from the horse race model it unfortunately adopted again during the Clinton administration's first year and a half of governing.

1/Campaign '92

To understand the relationship between the media and political
leadership over the past two years, it is necessary to briefly
review how those two institutions related during the campaign.
The press began the election year armed with good intentions not
to be taken in by what it sees as empty "photo-ops," manipulative
soundbites, and distorted advertising. But it quickly reverted to two
even more pervasive predilections: the emphasis on sensation and
horse race.

In her essay on the "subversive effects" of the press's "focus on
strategy" in *1-800-PRESIDENT*, the Twentieth Century Fund's report
on television and the 1992 campaign, scholar Kathleen Hall
Jamieson described why the media, in the face of twenty years of
scholarly and popular criticism, remained stubbornly absorbed in
this superficial, cynical, and ultimately alienating horse race model
of politics.[1]

The culture of sports, the need for changing story lines, cynicism
about the public and politics, fear of ideological challenge, and the
genuine mystery about who will win, all conspire to make the press
present politics as an exaggerated game between competing campaign
strategies. Jamieson also argued that this "strategy schema" has the
unfortunate consequence of distancing the public from politics and
the media. "The posture invited of the electorate by this schema is
cynical and detached . . . not 'Who is better able to serve as president?'
but 'Who is going to win?'" The relevant questions about what ideas
and policies candidates believe in and who would make a better president are crowded out.

If that is how the campaign began, the media were forced to
finally detach themselves from "the mindlessness" of the traditional

4

approach after the emergence of Ross Perot on CNN's "Larry King Live" in late February, journalist and author Ken Auletta argued in "On and Off the Bus: Lessons from Campaign '92."[2] Through Perot and New Media outlets like talk radio and Larry King, the public in a very real sense retrieved the campaign dialogue from the main-stream press. The public placed issues into the foreground of the campaign, the federal budget deficit for one, that were considered nonstarters by the two parties and by the press. Then in the fall, the mainstream press in reaction began to change its coverage to be more policy oriented, to focus less on the horse race, and to police the dialogue more.

Auletta saw the campaign as a play in three acts, with Act One, the early primaries, demonstrating all the evils that Jamieson had iden-tified. Act Two was the spring and fall, after the emergence of Perot, when the press had to react to the rise of New Media. But Act Three was still to play out, with many questions unresolved:

> We are in a transition . . . to what? Candidates and citizens alike had every reason to be irate about the insect-like behav-ior of the press. But without the filter of either a party or a vigilant press corps, there's a real danger candidates could snooker voters. . . . Technology is neutral. The true enemies are thoughtless candidates, thoughtless reporters and thoughtless citizens. Technology will permit future candi-dates to bypass the press more skillfully. But it is by no means certain this Brave New World has arrived.[3]

Auletta's questions were the right ones, and in "Let the Press Be the Press," scholar Thomas E. Patterson raised cautions against some of the very innovations the press seemed to be embracing as it tried to deal with its past failures and the rise of the New Media.[4] While the press, in reaction to how journalists felt they had been manipulated in the past, becomes an even more analytical and aggressive referee of campaigns, techniques Jamieson and Auletta partly endorse, Patterson reminded us of Walter Lippmann's still timely seventy-year-old admo-nition that the job of the press is to bring information to light, not to give it its larger meaning or order. That must be left to institutions and leaders, Lippmann wrote. If the press strays too far from the task of merely conveying what leaders are saying, it will get in the way of democracy, not advance it.

So what has happened since the campaign ended? Have the Old Media become increasingly obsolete and easily bypassed? Has technology allowed political leaders to more easily bamboozle the public? Has the public discourse coarsened because the media and the parties have further weakened as a filter, editor, and referee over the process? Are we moving closer to the chaos and mob psychology of instant electronic democracy?

2/Out with the Old

In April 1992, Clinton's third month in office, Sidney Blumenthal, Washington editor at *The New Yorker* magazine, wrote a lengthy "Letter from Washington" about the new White House and the press. In the grandest terms, Blumenthal declared the end of Old Media and the beginning of the new science of a more substantive, more precise form of communication by political leaders through targeted use of the New Media, new technology, and local reporters.[5]

The reason, in Blumenthal's view, was that Bill Clinton had learned to manipulate his message in a way that was entirely "new." He had "honed" the strategy of "narrowcasting" that began with shades and sax on Arsenio Hall's talk show, using new technology and specific media to reach the public with direct, targeted messages—"accurate, immediate and politically sensitive transmission of his policies." In this new world, "constituencies and legislators are targeted with precision, in media market after media market," with town hall–style gatherings, satellite feeds, direct interviews with administration officials, by flooding talk-radio shows, using the New Media to bypass the superficiality of the Old. And in its wake, "the national press" had begun "to suffer, at least a bit, the painful process known in the business world as disintermediation; that is, eliminating the middleman. What the President seeks is unmediated communication."[6]

"The Washington press corps will hardly disappear," he wrote, "but its old forms are in relative decline. . . . The world of the three-network media" had become "anachronistic. . . . The Big Media . . . are no more likely to make a triumphant return than are the big bands."[7]

Blumenthal was not the lone voice predicting the communications apocalypse. Inside the White House press room, where the reporters who covered the president toiled, the press corps wondered, too.

7

One reason journalists worried was the actions of the president himself. In his first fifteen weeks in office, Clinton held only two full, formal news conferences.[8] Of the past six presidents, only Ronald Reagan had held as few.[9] Clinton was more accessible than most presidents in taking questions at other public events, but reporters complained they were constrained from a wide-ranging inquiry by time limits or by the presence of other people on the stage, often visiting foreign leaders. The White House argued that, in all, Clinton had held fifteen press conferences during those fifteen weeks, but the press corps argued most of these were other events and so did not qualify as true press conferences. At this point in the discussion, the number is less significant than the fact that the press felt slighted. Clinton's true strategy is discussed later. The first lady was even more elusive to the mainstream press. By mid-April, she had done four "satellite tours," during which she granted interviews to TV anchors at nineteen different stations. But she had granted only three interviews to reporters from the national press.

Another reason for the myth that the White House thought of the establishment Washington press corps as obsolete and something to be bypassed was the age of so many of the staffers in Clinton's White House. With Clinton's arrival, the dress code from the Bush years requiring women to wear skirts gave way to open doors, open collars, and the sounds of Generation X rock groups like Front 242 and Radiohead around the Old Executive Office Building.[10] David Anderson, White House director of satellite services, was a twenty-three-year-old with spiked hair who dressed all in black and who was trying to finish his senior year at Oberlin College at night after work. The man responsible for Clinton's radio operations, Richard Strauss, was also twenty-three and finishing his senior year at UCLA by correspondence. Jess Sarmiento, whose job it was to get Clinton's message out through the ethnic, minority, and trade press, was twenty-three. Ernie Gibble, who handled local media from the Northeast, and Kim Hopper, who handled local media in the West, were twenty-seven. By one account, 63 of the 450 on the White House staff were younger than twenty-four. And overseeing them all as communications director was George Stephanopoulos, a brilliant, impatient, gum-chomping political operative, age thirty-two.

There was a genuine generation gap. Sixty-three-year-old David Broder of the *Washington Post* told the American Society of Newspaper Editors about how, after a particularly acrimonious phone conversation with Stephanopoulos, who was the same age as his son, Broder felt like telling the communications director to go to his room.[11] "As a father of a kid in college," a Reuters correspondent told me, "I find it somewhat off-putting to talk to male White House aides wearing earrings. It's like coming home and finding your kids got into the liquor cabinet."[12]

The kids came to represent the terrifying prospect of change, of Digital Democrats versus Analog Republicans, of satellites and computer databases instead of notebooks and intimate background briefings, of Bill Clinton's plastic Iron Man watch versus the heirloom timepiece that George Bush often wore, with different-colored canvas bands to match his different outfits.

Finally, the impression of bypass was reinforced because Jeff Eller, deputy assistant to the president and White House director of media affairs, and his staff were so much more creative than their predecessors under Bush. Strauss, the radio director, was appalled, for instance, to find such an antiquated radio "actuality line" at the White House for radio stations to receive daily feeds of quotes from the president and other key White House officials.[13] In the campaign, Strauss had rented a system in which two thousand radio stations could call at any one moment to pull soundbites from Clinton's campaign.[14] The ancient White House system could receive only three calls at a time.

Eller was amazed by the wiring inside the Old Executive Office Building because it was inadequate for computer lines. And the phone system was so old-fashioned that only a handful of officials had direct lines. Most calls went through a switchboard from the 1960s. It would not be until March 1994 that the White House was capable of having voice mail.[15]

Despite all this, however, those inside the White House supposedly responsible for the strategy of bypassing the Old Media read the accounts of their genius with bemusement. Clinton's staff may have been young and more interested in computers than were the Republicans who had been in office since the personal computer was in its infancy, but there was no strategy to govern the country by bypassing the national press.

What was happening was more mundane, and much more a sign of the administration's inexperience. One side of the White House Communications Department, the side that dealt with local and specialty media largely independently under Eller, was operating more competently than the other side, which dealt with the traditional White House press corps, under Eller's boss, George Stephanopoulos.

For instance, though Stephanopoulos and press secretary Dee Dee Myers briefed reporters three times a day in the first months—triple what the Bush White House did—Stephanopoulos defined his job in those briefings as a form of stonewalling rather than feeding the press. "Your job on the podium is to do nothing," he told me in an interview in March 1993. "Unless you decide to, you should not be making any news. You should not be trumping the President. You should not be getting ahead of him."[16]

Stephanopoulos spent much of his time with the national press, but, despite his enormous intelligence, his immaturity and his arrogance showed. It was not unheard of during interviews in his office for him to sit sideways in a chair with his feet dangling across the chair arm, and then simply jumping up and leaving in the middle, only to have his secretary come in and say, "I'm sorry, George has left. I guess your interview is over."[17]

Calls were not returned in time for journalists to meet their deadlines. And in a way White House reporters found insulting, Stephanopoulos and others around him seemed never to acknowledge even the most trivial mistakes; reporters have repeatedly complained that they felt he was never leveling with them. Some degree of "spin" and political hype is necessary and expected in the White House, but most in the press corps felt here it was unrelenting and excessive. And that made it unconvincing. "George felt he could talk his way out of anything," as one of his friends in the White House put it.[18] Or as ABC correspondent Brit Hume described it, "These guys definitely believe in the efficacy of spin."[19]

All administrations consider the press a necessary, dangerous, and often infuriatingly irresponsible institution. And Stephanopoulos's goal in dealing with journalists was similar to his predecessors'. Before taking office, the young communications director, in fact, met with several former White House press secretaries and media advisers. They told him that the key to a successful presidency was control, maintaining the agenda, maintaining the focus. "My discussions with the Clinton people were mostly about how you maintain the focus," Michael Deaver said. "When the president gives up the agenda he is lost."[20] Another informal adviser before the Clintons took office, David Gergen, agreed. The Clinton team was trying to improve on the techniques of the Reagan team, "like the Japanese who studied American quality and then beat our brains out with it."[21]

Stephanopoulos thought keeping the national press corps at bay was the way to maintain control. That was his interest: control, not bypass.

But his way of doing it struck most journalists as arrogant and sometimes incompetent. The best-known incident was the decision in the first week to ban the White House press corps from the Upper Press Office, an alcove outside Stephanopoulos's and Myers's offices. The change had logic. The press room is situated between the Oval Office and the residence, and the press secretary's office itself is just across from the Oval Office. And Stephanopoulos, who was a close adviser to the president, wanted to move freely into the Oval Office without being questioned by the press about it. Reagan aides considered the location a problem, too. But Michael Deaver had proposed the same change twelve years earlier when Ronald Reagan took office, and those with White House experience working for Reagan persuaded him that doing so would be a mistake. Once the press corps had been given a perk, they said, it could never be taken away without a big fight.[22] But there were no such old White House hands to so advise Stephanopoulos.

In addition to lack of experience, the youthful self-confidence and impatience that the White House staff displayed was not limited to its dealings with the press. "They barely conceal the idea sometimes that they consider the older Democrats around town as losers," said one prominent Democrat. Added another, an old friend of Clinton's, about Stephanopoulos in particular, "You will be talking to George on the phone and 'click,' he will just hang up on you. The arrogance is unbelievable."[23]

Los Angeles Times White House reporter David Lauter probably put it best during these early months. "They're not ignoring us" in the national press. "They're dissing us," showing, in the language of youth, lack of respect.[24]

Shortcomings of basic competence, political judgment, and simple understanding of human nature could be seen in such embarrassments as the $200 haircut Clinton received sitting in a plane on a runway at the Los Angeles International Airport while the press corps waited. As former Reagan and Bush aide Margaret Tutwiler explained later, "Someone on the plane with the press should have said, 'We can't sit here. If we do, the press will ask why are we sitting here. That is their job. And we don't want to have to tell them it's because the President is getting a $200 haircut. So let's go.'"[25]

The travel office fiasco, too, while partly an attempt to reward friends with jobs in the travel office and perhaps even line the pockets of political supporters with air charter contracts, was partly a sign of basic incompetence in handling the press. One of the motivations for firing the travel office staff, according to White House documents, was that those people were deemed too friendly with the press corps.

By the end of May, when the haircut and the travel office story combined back-to-back, the Clinton administration found itself under the awkward burden of having to prove that it was not incompetent. Stephanopoulos's crew had become the brunt of jokes. Even mannerly Ted Koppel on "Nightline," sitting incredulously as Stephanopoulos tried to fend off criticisms and counterattack critics of the travel office fiasco, suggested that Stephanopoulos's behavior was so misguided that he wondered if the presidential aide was "into pain."[26]

The most inept White House staff he had seen in twenty-four years in Washington, *Wall Street Journal* columnist and TV personality Al Hunt proclaimed on one of his weekend talk TV shows.[27]

Even in early interviews, the people supposedly involved in devising the strategy of bypassing the press seemed surprised that this idea had become so powerful.

"All this stuff about us skipping the national media is great," said David Anderson, the kid with the spiked hair who conceives of and arranges most of Clinton's local satellite TV appearances. "It makes the local media outlets we are trying to woo happy. And it isn't true."[28] Anderson's boss, Eller, sounded ironic about the idea of the media's obsolescence. "Sure, the national press are like a dinosaur. They're huge, and they will be around for another million years."[29]

Stephanopoulos understood this, too. "The press's perspective is hardly irrelevant," he explained during this period, "but it is no longer the whole story."[30]

In short, the White House understood the simple mathematical laws of communications. The government could not govern the country by town hall or talk show alone. There were simply too many local TV and radio stations to make such a strategy possible. Nor could the American people realistically watch the government—live—on C-SPAN and edit for themselves. They still had to rely on the mainstream press to do it for them. Roughly thirty million households still tuned into the three network evening newscasts each night (not to mention the ten million who watched the morning network news shows each day). That was still more Americans than watched any other single news outlet, and the White House could reach them by servicing three journalists. True, life had changed. Where work in the Reagan White House literally was suspended at 6:30 each night while the network news shows were on the air, in the Clinton White House meetings were scheduled and continued during the news hour. White House officials had already seen on CNN how the press was reacting to events, they told me, and the networks were not the force they once were. In a sense, there were now too many forces for people to possibly keep track of. But a close look at precisely what the Clinton administration was doing with the New Media reveals that there was no strategy to bypass the Old Media. Far from it.

3/USING THE NEW MEDIA

By the end of February 1994, a year after a taking office, Clinton had conducted 161 interviews with local television journalists from around the country. The other principals in the administration did even fewer interviews with local television. Vice President Al Gore in the first year in office did 76 local TV interviews. The first lady did 26. For Clinton, that averages out to three a week, far less than the frequency with which he appears through the national press. And most of these interviews, as we shall see, took place at a handful of group sessions or while Clinton was traveling, techniques that hardly constitute anything new or striking.[31]

By contrast, President Clinton in his first year held forty-five news conferences with the national press, the most of any president in modern history. Moreover, the frequency did not change after June 1993, the point at which Clinton's relations with the national press supposedly began to improve.[32] All told, Clinton in his first year did twelve more press conferences than Bush, the president who had held the most news conferences of any modern president, thirty-eight more than Ronald Reagan, twenty-two more than Jimmy Carter, twenty-eight more than Gerald Ford, and thirty-six more than Richard Nixon. Twenty-one of these news conferences were joint appearances with visiting foreign leaders. The rest, twenty-four, were alone with the press corps. In addition, Clinton had arranged dozens of lunches and dinners with reporters, and tended to take questions at other appearances, so much so that some critics began to complain that Clinton was cheapening the currency of being president through overexposure. *Time* magazine White House correspondent Michael Duffy, one of the most respected reporters covering the president, stopped attending many White House events because, he said, the president made himself so available, most of them were no longer particularly newsworthy. Instead, he found himself usually reading the transcripts.[33]

The idea of bypass is a myth.

A close look at what the Clinton administration was doing, indeed, will help demonstrate why bypass would be so difficult. The most familiar modern method of reaching out to the public beyond the White House press corps is the satellite media tour—sitting in an office in Washington and conducting interviews via satellite with local TV reporters and anchors who are back at their studios around the country. In fact, President Clinton did little of this in his first year. Only 12 of his 161 interviews with local television were satellite sessions from Washington. The technique is an inefficient way of communicating because there are six hundred TV stations in the country, and the White House has no budget for satellite work and has to beg and borrow the money from various contingency funds or from federal agencies.[34]

The bulk of Clinton's reaching out to local media involved his doing what the White House calls "one-on-ones," in which the president would, while traveling, grant exclusive interviews with local television stations. This age-old method of reaching out accounted for seventy-six of Clinton's interviews with local television his first year—nearly half—yet it amounts to little more than what Abraham Lincoln would have done with local newspapermen while traveling in his day, or Franklin Roosevelt with radio and newspapers more than a half century ago. [35]

One genuine innovation, the inspiration of twenty-three-year-old college student Anderson, was what the administration calls "Video Press Conferences." This amounts to using satellites to allow local reporters in targeted states, without commuting to Washington, to conduct a free-ranging press conference with the president, just as the White House press corps does in person. The White House would invite reporters from every news organization in a state to the studios of one TV station, where reporters could see and hear the president on a TV monitor and he could see and hear them. The questioners and questions were not screened. The only difference between this and an in-person press conference was that the order of questioning was determined in advance by random drawing. The president would stand at a lectern in a small TV studio, Room 456 in the corner of the Old Executive Office Building. And on a few TV stations in the targeted state, including the host station, the entire half-hour press conference would be carried live, preempting regular daytime programming.[36]

As intriguing as the idea is, the White House conducted only five of these events, reaching Arizona, California, Louisiana, Nevada, and Wisconsin, mostly to promote the Clinton budget plan in July 1993. All told, he took questions from thirty TV stations, plus dozens more from newspaper, magazine, and radio reporters during these five sessions, and earned saturation coverage in the home states. But the number of these was limited, according to Media Affairs Director Eller, because the conferences are costly given the virtually nonexistent budget for this type of work, because the president's time is so limited, and because there are more efficient ways of delivering his message.[37]

Monitoring these sessions inside Room 456 at the Old Executive Office Building, I discovered an interesting trend. In general, smaller news organizations tended to ask more policy-oriented questions, while the larger local media organizations tended to ask more political questions. The political reporter from the *Arizona Republic*, the state's largest newspaper, for instance, asked how big a political setback it would be for the president if his deficit reduction plan didn't pass Congress. "It would be a big setback for America," Clinton answered. "They think they're being tough," Eller mused afterward, "but those are the easiest questions of all."[38]

The question from the tiny *Sun City Daily News* in Sun City, Arizona, was harder. Most of his readers are retirees, the reporter said, so how did Clinton's budget help senior citizens? In answering a question that was fairly specific, and since his plan didn't go out of its way to help seniors, Clinton staggered a bit. "A lot of senior citizens who have their investments in primarily interest-earning accounts have had their earnings drop as interest rates have gone down. . . . I think it will strengthen their investments," he said vaguely, "by promoting economic growth." The answer was a bit hypocritical, since Clinton had been regularly stumping in front of the national press by saying that he had helped boost the economy by keeping interest rates down.

The White House also experimented with another interesting innovation: The day after the introduction of the health care plan, it staged a satellite press briefing for journalists in locations in all fifty states. The first lady and other top officials gave a two-hour briefing on the plan, in effect providing local journalists on this occasion with the same detail and the same high-ranking officials as the national press. The same week, the administration gave a similar briefing to radio talk show hosts invited to the White House, and the next day allowed the radio hosts to broadcast from the White House lawn, where administration officials wandered from show to show answering questions.

The administration also experimented with a handful of so-called regional addresses when the president had something significant to say to a part of the country but chose for whatever reason not to deliver a nationwide address. He delivered one to the people of California, for instance, during the wildfires in the fall of 1993.[39]

Finally, the president staged five town hall meetings in his first year, two to support the introduction of health-care reform, one focused on children, and two early ones on no particular subjects at all. Those first two came in March and late May, both times when the president was unable to get his message out through the mainstream press. In March, he was suffering criticism for gays in the military. Late May came while the press was focused on the haircut and the travel mess. "There is no set time, or schedule about when you use them," Eller said. "It is as the situation warrants." The nation was hardly being governed by Larry King.

(In March–April 1994, a strange phenomenon developed. In March, the president held a prime-time White House press conference dominated by questions about his involvement in the Whitewater land deal in Arkansas. Two weeks later Clinton did a town hall in Charlotte, during which several voters asked questions that were noticeably more aggressive than the ones the press had asked earlier. Generally, voters tend to be more polite and less aggressive than reporters. This reversal of form raises the question of whether the press has become defensive about its role, while voters are becoming more accustomed to asking leaders questions directly and thereby are more aggressive. As this paper focuses largely on Clinton's first year and does not examine Whitewater specifically, the phenomenon is beyond the scope of this study but deserves watching.)

By the second year of the Clinton presidency, the White House also began providing regular live satellite feeds of presidential events in their entirety to local TV stations around the country, particularly when the president took out-of-town trips. When the president went in March 1994 to Miami to speak with senior citizens about health care, some portion of the feed of the event was carried by eighty different stations.[40] The idea offers local stations the chance to see, air, or edit the president for themselves. Currently, the networks and CNN don't generally send local stations around the country the entire feed of presidential events. Instead, the locals usually receive news packages prepared for them by the networks' affiliate services, or they pick up stories that aired on CNN or on the network shows, which they often reedit and narrate with their own anchor.[41]

These live, full-run feeds get close to Eller's vision of how the White House might operate in the future. He would like to see a White House satellite and cable channel, on which all presidential events are carried live in their entirety, available not only to TV stations but to any viewer who wants to tune in at home. For now, this is the closest the White House can come realistically to bypassing the mainstream press. But even this would be limited by the number of local stations that want to air or edit these events for themselves.

The Republican party in much the same way offered George Bush's campaign stops to local stations during the 1992 election, but it never knew how many of these feeds were aired. In fall 1993, the Clinton White House began to be able to monitor usage by stations because of new technology that makes it possible to track who has downlinked the image off the satellite. The technology is still expensive enough that the White House is doing it only occasionally. But the technology means politicians can measure who is watching their feeds, and that there is a way to measure how much appetite there is for local TV stations to watch presidential events and edit them for themselves or even air them live.

Altogether, then, this fairly modest use of the New Media amounts to interesting experiments, not wholesale bypass. In the end, the myth of Old versus New Media in some respects is a false dichotomy. Rather than bypassing the Old, the Clinton administration found that while it was experimenting with the New Media, it also had to service the Old—to feed it information, massage the journalists, and understand the press's needs in order to manage its message through the press filter. Rather than giving politicians more tools to control the media, technology had made the task more complex. Not only were there simply more media outlets to control, but as we will see in the next section, the New Media also were changing the rules of news. And in reaction the Old Media were changing in ways that made it even more difficult to manage one's message.

4/Learning to Manage the Old Media

The Clinton administration's relationship with the mainstream press, and its coverage on television, began to improve in July 1993, one month after the White House communications staff was reorganized under David Gergen.

The reason was not so much that the Clinton administration changed its strategy about how to treat the mainstream press. It simply changed tactics. After six months of great effort but not a good deal of common sense or good manners, the administration finally began using the time-tested techniques for handling the national press that presidents had employed for generations—courtesy, flattery, and, whenever possible, access.

Among the first moves, George Stephanopoulos was removed as communications director, and replaced by former deputy chief of staff Mark Gearan, who had been campaign press secretary for Democratic presidential candidate Michael Dukakis in 1988. Thereafter:

▲ Calls were returned before deadline, whereas Stephanopoulos and others had been tied up in late afternoon meetings and often didn't call back, reporters relate, until after deadline. That meant the White House's full explanation was often not contained in stories.[42]

▲ Press Secretary Dee Dee Myers was included more regularly in the president's daily morning briefing by senior staff, which made her more helpful when talking to reporters and made reporters feel they were getting better treatment.[43]

▲ The character of the daily press briefings provided something newsworthy rather than simply allowing reporters to ask

questions that yielded no usable answers, a tactic that had put
the communications staff at odds with the press corps.[44]

▲   New communications director Gearan was more respectful
     and polite in his manner, more candid about some of his
     answers, and more modest in the amount of "spin" or
     rhetorical insistence that he provided.[45]

▲   Gearan began also using the White House briefing room for
     helpful background briefings by senior White House aides
     from other parts of the administration.

▲   Finally, the president himself spent more time with
     reporters, hosting lunches, dinners, even picnics on the
     White House lawn—all of which allowed reporters to see his
     human side and hear the reasoning behind his decisions
     firsthand.

"We had left the impression we didn't care much about the White
House press corps," Gearan said in October. "That wasn't true, but
that was the impression."[46]

The changes resulted in more positive press coverage for several
reasons. By returning calls and answering questions in ways that were
more timely, the administration was getting its full explanation of
events into stories. By giving reporters the impression they were being
treated with more respect—that they weren't being "dissed"—the
administration tended to receive from them the benefit of the doubt.
By using the briefing room to supply reporters with usable information—by servicing the press in these sessions, if you will—the White
House was better able to shape stories.

Consider the week in late July that the administration announced
its final plan for gays in the military. Four days before the plan was
formally announced, the administration conducted detailed briefings for reporters at the White House and Pentagon explaining the
plan in detail. Secretary of Defense Les Aspin followed up those briefings by personally phoning reporters from key news organizations to
supply their stories with "exclusive" quotes. These sessions were conducted on Friday, and the plan was described as "tentative" so that
the weekend talk shows could not dissect the plan too definitively,
since it could still change before being announced on Monday. The

subsequent coverage from the administration's point of view could not have been better. "Chiefs Back Clinton and Gay-Troop Plan," read the *New York Times* headline. "A Step for Gay Soldiers but Not for Gay Rights," read the *Los Angeles Times*. This was precisely the message the administration wanted to send, one high official conceded. The headlines read as if the White House press office had written them for itself.

Was the improved coverage entirely a function of press management? Clearly not.

For the purposes of this paper I used studies by the Center for the Media and Public Affairs in Washington, which conducted content analysis of the coverage of the White House on weekday nightly newscasts of the three broadcast networks plus CNN.

Through June, the center concluded, only one-third of the evaluations of Clinton on the three TV networks' nightly new shows were positive.[47] That compares with 55 percent positive for George Bush's first year. (Bush cultivated and flattered the White House press corps and benefited from being more able to answer their questions than his predecessor, Ronald Reagan. With an experienced White House largely inherited from Reagan, moreover, Bush's first year was free of some of the early mistakes of Clinton's. Public approval of Clinton's performance, coincidentally, fell with the coverage, from 60 percent positive in March to 37 percent in June.)[48]

In summer, the coverage began to improve, from 27 percent positive in May to 40 percent in July. And by November through January 1994, it was consistently near or above 50 percent positive, higher than during Clinton's first month in office.

The improved handling of the national media helped, but it was far from the only factor.

In June, Clinton made a well-received choice for the Supreme Court. In July, he handled himself well on a trip to Tokyo and secured passage of his budget by Congress. In September, he delivered a half-improvised but widely acclaimed speech on health care to Congress. These policy successes, which were real, drove the coverage.

In late fall and winter, however, Clinton began to lose momentum on health care, delaying the introduction of the legislation and losing support in Congress, and the coverage slipped again to just 30 percent positive.

Then in late December and early January, the press began asking questions about alleged sexual liaisons and then about Clinton's involvement in the Whitewater land deal. Those questions subsided during the president's European summit, but they resurfaced with a vengeance in March, after reports that the Rose law firm had shredded documents belonging to Deputy White House Counsel Vince Foster, after Assistant Attorney General Webster Hubbell had to resign amid allegations of financial misconduct, and after revelations that administration officials had held meetings that raised questions about whether the White House was trying to influence the investigation into Whitewater.

So events, not simply communications strategy, played the dominant role in how the administration was covered, and in public approval of the president.

But as events of the first six months of 1993 and the cold winter of 1994 would reveal, the Old Media had also changed in ways that made their relationship more difficult than anything the Bush or Reagan administrations had had to deal with.

5/THE OLD MEDIA REACT TO THE NEW

Before 1992, journalists liked to think that politicians sought out talk shows, local media, and call-in programs to avoid the kind of probing questions that trained, national reporters asked.[49]

But in 1992, that idea was obliterated. Journalists recognized that the New Media were gaining influence because the public, not politicians, was repudiating the way the Old Media operated. The public was rejecting politics cut up into small bits, the focus on horse race over policy, the fascination with polling and tactics. It was no coincidence that the first time any presidential candidate was interviewed live and alone on national television for an hour was on "Larry King Live." The mainstream press no longer offered candidates that platform.

Journalists also saw that the public watched and listened to the New Media because programs like "Larry King Live" allowed people to shape the agenda and to ask questions for themselves. And journalists recognized that they were failing to ask all the questions the public wanted answered.

The public learned about a wider variety of issues from these programs—and from the network programs on those days when they converted themselves to call-in formats—than it did from the traditional programs. And many of the most memorable and meaningful moments of the campaign came during these New Media formats rather than the traditional political programs. It was on the "Phil Donahue Show" that a woman who did not support Bill Clinton told the talk show host he should be ashamed for harping on Clinton's marital fidelity, instead of spending time on substantive policy subjects.[50]

Even more troubling to traditional journalists, the 1992 campaign was a challenge to the standing of the mainstream press as a credible surrogate for the public in general. Journalists had become part of the elite establishment from which the public felt alienated. The press was part of what was wrong with politics. And this alienation went deeper than the notion that a few disaffected conservatives had gravitated to talk radio to vent their rage. Big-time journalists had little in common anymore with their audiences. Reporters were celebrities, even millionaires, the kind of people written about on society pages, who appeared on TV talk shows, such as CNN's "Capitol Gang," as equals of the politicians they covered, referring to one other by first name and rendering opinions about how the president should or should not behave. The press had become players, pundits, celebrities, not reporters observing and reporting primarily for the folks back home.

During the fall of 1992, members of the mainstream press adapted to the rise of the New Media by recognizing their isolation and deferring to public anger about the process. ABC anchor Peter Jennings expressed concern to his network colleagues that he felt out of touch with the public sentiment about the campaign.[51] ABC's "World News Tonight" turned over its daily five-minute American Agenda segment to a comparison of the candidates' policy positions, followed a focus group of undecided voters each Friday in a long discussion of the campaign, and sent its chief political correspondent Jim Wooten on the road to cover the campaign through the eyes of average voters rather than by following the candidates. "The CBS Evening News" examined the campaign one day a week from a different city around the country and introduced a daily campaign segment entitled Reality Check, during which it analyzed the truth of claims contained in candidates' ads and rhetoric.[52]

In addition, the *Charlotte Observer* in North Carolina and the *Wichita Eagle* in Kansas moved away from traditional journalistic definitions of political news and oriented their coverage instead around questions from voters or around issues that voters told them they were most concerned with.

Since the election, however, the press has changed from the path it was following in the fall of 1992. Three trends are discernible.

▲   The press has returned to the horse race model of coverage, emphasizing politics over policy, and focusing on who is winning and who is losing.

▲   The press has reacted to the rise of the New Media not by
     returning to basics but actually by becoming more subjec-
     tive and quicker to exercise its political judgments than
     before.

▲   There is growing evidence that the rise of the New Media is
     continuing to add pressure for lowering the standards of the
     mainstream press, making it more likely that rumor and
     innuendo will be printed or aired and pushing the press fur-
     ther in the direction of tabloidization.

     Let's take them one at a time.[53]

6/RETURN TO HORSE RACE COVERAGE

The press's return to making horse race reporting the focus of much of its coverage of politics was startlingly demonstrated by the fact that within two days of the U.S. bombing of Iraq in March of 1993 in retaliation for the assassination plot against George Bush, ABC and the *Washington Post* had conducted a public opinion survey to analyze the effect of the bombing on Bill Clinton's popularity.

This emphasis on politics rather than on governance is embedded in the coverage in several ways. Even more so than with print, a close study of the network stories over Clinton's first year reveals that the TV coverage has tended to be event-driven, rather than being driven by the policies or ideas that Clinton is trying to advance. Hence, while there are exceptions, policy initiatives generally tend to be covered only when they are formally sent to the Hill, voted on, during a hearing, or when someone attacks them. This tends to lead to more episodic and potentially confusing coverage of policy, particularly policy that relates to such long-term issues as welfare reform, or the stimulus package, or deficit reduction—addressing these issues only at moments when there is a news event to hang it on.

This orientation toward events also suggests, despite arguments by Clinton advisers to the contrary, that a president who delivers important speeches or stages dramatic events to illustrate his policy initiatives can make more headway with television than the Clinton team came to believe during the campaign. But those events have to be substantive, and the speeches meaningful. Interestingly, Clinton advisers in interviews with me have continually suggested that they think the press won't cover such events anymore because they are viewed as photo-ops. I think the key is that the president has to have something significant to say.

The coverage on television, as is true in print, also shows a bias toward conflict: young Democrats say they won't vote for the president's stimulus package; military leaders hate the idea of allowing gays in the military. The event-driven nature of the coverage encourages this because it focuses on ideas not as ideas but as conflicts in the political arena. To some degree it was ever thus in journalism, of course. A good fight between neighbors is a story, while people on the block getting along is not. But without questioning the wisdom of this journalistic convention, it does appear that the press's conflict orientation is intensifying, for several reasons. We are in a period, as occurs cyclically, of more weakened social and political consensus now than was true during the cold war. Hence our politics has become more rancorous than it has been at certain periods in the past. I think the proliferation of the media, furthermore, tends to encourage this rancor. With so many media out there, political consultants often point out, it is increasingly difficult to develop a message that rises above or gets remembered through the din. One way a politician can get remembered and get coverage is to be particularly provocative. I think, too, that political actors in Washington—politicians and interest groups—have become more expert in the science of manipulating the media by knowing the norms and conventions of the press. And as seniority on Capitol Hill has given way to other sources of power, the politician with the knack for making waves and making news gains more authority, such as Republican congressman Newt Gingrich of Georgia, Democratic congressman John Dingell of Michigan, or Democratic senator John Breaux of Louisiana.

Once again, in other words, the press magnifies and shapes events it is covering by the act of observation. The press's conflict orientation, in short, makes politics more rancorous. This conflict orientation also tends to make the coverage more vulnerable to manipulation by political opponents wielding criticism. That is one reason, for instance, that a politician skilled at the rough one-liner, such as Republican senator Bob Dole of Kansas or Republican senator Alfonse D'Amato of New York, can stand out. And finally, the focus on conflict encourages writing about politics rather than policy.

The emphasis on politics versus governance is further encouraged by the traditional formats employed by the media, like television's two-minute stories and ten-second soundbites. It is difficult to examine policy in such time periods. The problem, moreover, is only made more difficult by the growing sense among television executives that the public cannot handle complex issues unless they relate direct-ly to areas of personal interest such as health or personal finance.

Finally, the press has tended to focus on three basic and some-times intersecting story lines about Clinton that have been ongoing. The first was that Clinton did not ever fully level with people, that on some level perhaps he was incapable of it. This basic idea about Clinton was established in his relationship with the press going back to the New Hampshire primary, where most reporters, even those who interviewed Clinton at length, felt that he had failed to level with peo-ple over Gennifer Flowers and the draft, even while he was claiming full disclosure. He was "Slick Willie," the guy who thought he could talk his way out of anything, the guy who tried to deny he had ever tried marijuana by denying he had ever broken the laws of his country; the guy who, when finally cornered, admitted that he had tried pot in England but then claimed he hadn't inhaled. Now any time Clinton's actions did not live up to his rhetoric, the story had greater coverage because it seemed to attach itself to a larger issue about the president.

The second related idea about Clinton that drove coverage was that he was different ideologically—perhaps more liberal—from what he claimed during the campaign. Finally, the third notion about Clinton was that he would compromise too easily on virtually any-thing. There was no issue, no point, over which he would stand on principle and say no.

All three of these ideas converged to help fuel the extraordinary coverage of gays in the military, a story that dominated the network reporting of the first two months of Clinton's presidency. Would he live up to his promise to allow gays in the military? Or would he dodge a tough issue? If he was pushing this, was he more liberal than he claimed? Or would he compromise? The tendency of the press to find fault, combined with the negative impressions Clinton had left from the campaign, made this an almost no-win issue with the press. And that seemed to make Clinton's elevation of the issue appear political-ly all the more inept.

Such ideas, which reporters may harbor privately about politi-cians, have always shaped coverage, but they may be even more important today. Across the media, there is more emphasis than ever on what might be called "thematic" approach to the news, connecting stories to larger preexisting trends and ideas. In television, this is occurring partly because the networks have been forced to cut back on resources for hard news, particularly in Washington. With fewer staff to cover the news, there is less original reporting than there once was and a greater value on reporters who can get on the air frequently and who can package stories expertly and attractively. Stories are even often referred to now as "packages," a term borrowed from local news. This thematic approach also helps explain stories to a public that journalists fear is not attuned to public affairs. And as we will see below, this thematic approach intersects with another change in the press.

7/THE ERA OF SUBJECTIVITY

O ne of the most significant movements in journalism today is a broad shift toward becoming quicker to render judgments, more subjective in the tone of news stories, and to base those judgments more easily on reporters' own authority rather than on reporting attributed to outside experts. The shift toward interpretive, analytical, and judgmental reporting is based on many factors, some of them legitimate and well founded. But the movement is not well thought out, and some of the interpretive reporting goes much too far. Taken as a whole, it amounts to a new era of subjectivity.

A two-month study I conducted of the front pages of the *New York Times, Los Angeles Times,* and *Washington Post*[54] revealed that:

▲   Only slightly more than half of the 1,332 stories that ran in the spring of 1993 could be classified as straight news.

▲   Nearly 40 percent were analytical or interpretative treatment of news events or trends.

▲   Nearly 80 percent of these analytical stories had no label identifying them as analysis, interpretation, or opinion. (About 5 percent of the front-page stories were features, and another 5 percent were special projects.)

The move toward more interpretive reporting reflects longstanding cultural changes and changing technology. Today's more skeptical public would not be satisfied with the credulous coverage of the 1950s and 1960s when the quotes of public figures went unchallenged. And in an era of twenty-four-hour news, newspapers feel compelled to provide context, perspective, and interpretation, since they infer that many of their audience are already familiar with the basic facts.

But as journalists have tried to cope with the rise of the New Media, the trend toward interpretation has accelerated noticeably. The task of having something "new" to add on the show that evening or in the paper the next morning has become more difficult and intense as mainstream press swim more self-consciously in the rising river of radio talk shows, TV punditry, C-SPAN seminars, and after-noon chat. And many journalists have begun to strain to have some-thing provocative to say.

On the White House beat, "a lot of what we do is what I call souf-flé journalism," said *Los Angeles Times* White House correspondent John M. Broder, describing a recipe that calls for one part informa-tion mixed with two parts attitude and two parts conjecture. And after twenty-four hours or so, the analysis it contains has fallen flat.[55]

Even reporters are surprised by the freedom they now are accord-ed by their editors. In its coverage of Clinton's budget plan, for instance, *Los Angeles Times* economics correspondent James Risen admits, "We definitely are willing to write what we think about this budget in a way we were not, say, in the budget package of 1990." Consider the language in one Risen piece: "A few simple statistics go a long way toward explaining why the [Clinton budget deficit plan] may not work, despite the best intentions of its authors," it began.

While interpretive reporting is arguably the highest form of jour-nalism, it is also the most demanding, and there are three serious problems with the way some of the new subjectivity is currently prac-ticed. First, much of the analysis the press is capable of in a matter of hours is not meaningful and seems hyperventilated.

Witness the judgments on *Time* magazine's covers over the first eight months of 1993. On January 25, three weeks after Clinton became Man of the Year, *Time* put a heroic Clinton on the cover under the head-line "Stand and Deliver: With tough choices at home and a dangerous world abroad Bill Clinton takes charge." A week later, *Time*'s cover declared "Clinton's First Blunder," referring to the withdrawal of his attorney general-designate. A month after that, *Time* was invoking the ambition of Clinton's agenda again with the cover headline "You Say You Want a Revolution." Yet two weeks after that the cover was "Anguish over Bosnia: Will it be Clinton's Vietnam?" On June 1, *Time* declared Clinton "The Incredible Shrinking President." Nine weeks later, it was extolling the enormity of Clinton's agenda again: "Overturning the

Reagan Era: It's painful, messy and modest, but Clinton's budget signals a new course for America."

The speed with which journalists make these judgments has become breathtaking. Ten days into Clinton's term, ABC's Jeff Greenfield even did a story mocking how many journalists already had declared Clinton's administration a failure.

Increasingly, the new subjectivity also tends to focus on predicting the future rather than explaining or understanding the past. This kind of speculative reporting is often wrong and usually less helpful than the harder work of true interpretive journalism, which is grounded in explaining what has happened, not what will happen. When the fiery end came for the Branch Davidian cult in Waco, Texas, the *Wall Street Journal*'s lead story the next day suggested Waco could be Clinton's Bay of Pigs, a policy disaster that defined John F. Kennedy's first months in office as often incompetent. Or again, there was *Time*'s "Anguish over Bosnia" cover: behind Clinton was a black-and-white photo of an anguished Lyndon Johnson.

Since it is increasingly based on shorter amounts of time, moreover, not enough of this interpretive work is grounded in true reporting. An alarming number of the stories in the newspaper study showed that the analysis was based rather on the judgments of the journalist, and this journalistic expertise tends to be political rather than substantive. So much of the discussion, rather than concerning itself with policymaking or governing, focused on politics or management style— matters that are safe and subjective and not prone to be challenged for ideological or reportorial bias. On the eve of Clinton's first vacation in August 1993, for instance, the *New York Times* front-page analysis took stock of his presidency so far by revealing, in breathless tones, that Clinton was disorganized: "The triumphs and wreckage now scattered across his calendar reflect what he himself brought to the Presidency. More by nature than by circumstance, perhaps, Mr. Clinton governs by careening from one tight spot to another."

Scoops, in this age, become a matter of who can be first with a new angle on something rather than new information. Around Washington some reporters even use the term *scoops of perception.* And this chase to be first with new angles puts a premium on being provocative and interesting, but not necessarily right. "Often wrong but never in doubt," a smiling Dan Rather often scolds the press.

"Wisdom is who can be first to cast a judgment on a surfing level," admits *Los Angeles Times* political correspondent Ronald Brownstein.

"And the result is a careening back and forth. It implies more motion than exists. We are constantly breaking stories in both directions."[56]

In some cases, the new subjectivity does not so much mean being first with a new perception as it does adding "edge" or "attitude" to the story. A lot of this analysis is journalists trying to imitate the evocative writing of Maureen Dowd of the *New York Times*. Rather than being oriented toward analyzing policy, Dowd's work emphasizes sensibility. Her focus is a president's style and her own personal reaction to it. Her eye is idiosyncratic, not ideological: I like this, I don't like that. And the power of her writing lies not in the information she provides but in her turn of phrase, syntax as insight. She is the columnist as newswriter. In Dowd's hand, this often works because her eye and her writing are extraordinary. Of Clinton she would write one of the most memorable summaries: "What you see never turns out to be exactly what you get. The kinks are never quite ironed out. The status is never quo. . . . The man who merely chews on his stogies has given us the Presidency as exploding cigar . . . he's the first president as gifted adolescent."

Dowd's many imitators, however, usually fall painfully short. When the president vacationed in Martha's Vineyard in August 1993, for instance, the *Washington Post* White House correspondent tried a little edge about the presidential golf game. She even employed imaginary quotations. "Today he is wearing an all-lavender get up so doofy looking, so White Guy, that you just know Chelsea took one disgusted teen-age glance and rolled her eyes, 'Oh Daddy, you're not wearing that.'"

The networks, which were quicker to allow reporters freedom to offer personal feelings into their coverage years ago, similarly feel the pressure from New Media to provide analysis. The basic structure of the evening newscasts since 1989, indeed, has been to group two and sometimes three pieces about the main story of the day at the top of the broadcast, a combination that allows the newscast to provide for as much as ten minutes on a single subject. ABC, in particular, has followed this structure. The approach is based, in part, on the assumption that viewers have already heard the basic facts of the news even before 6:30 P.M., so the networks must now provide viewers with analysis and larger perspective on the news. This is a prospect that may seem unlikely to critics of television, but it often works well. And recognizing the change is essential to understanding network TV news. The assumption is based partly on the fact that the networks have been forced to offer their local affiliates their footage before the networks themselves use it on the air. It is an assumption, too, based on the fact that more people now watch local news than networks, and that the news day begins at 5:30 A.M. in many markets and continues, via cable and a proliferating spectrum of news and talk radio stations, throughout the day.

8/THE NEW MEDIA HAVE LOWERED JOURNALISTIC STANDARDS

If the return to horse race journalism and the press's increasing subjectivity make the relationship between government and the media more difficult, so does the third change in the press since the election of 1992: The New Media are helping lower the Old Media's ethical standards.

There are several cases to suggest that rumor and innuendo now find their way into the press and public dialogue more easily than they once did. Consider, for instance, how in March 1994 conservative interests succeeded in peddling the idea that Deputy White House Counsel Vince Foster's suicide was linked to the Whitewater land deal. It began when a right-wing group sent a fax newsletter to news organizations around the country passing a rumor that Foster had actually died at a White House "safe house" and was later moved to the park in Virginia. The rumor was attributed to unnamed sources in Democratic senator Daniel Patrick Moynihan's office, which later denied the allegation. But radio talk show host Rush Limbaugh picked up the rumor and repeated it over the air that day. So did others, among them a talk show host in Florida who freely suggested that the report, which was now relayed as more than a rumor, raised the specter that Foster's death was not a suicide but murder. The rumor, now conveyed over radio, provided an opportunity for some stock market speculators to make a little profit by trading on gossip. And the next day the *Washington Post* business section ran a story about the rumor on the grounds that it had moved the stock market. The episode is only one example among many, but it represents a significant change in press standards.

The change was visible during the 1992 campaign. Because they were able to level their musings about the trip over C-SPAN and provoke Larry King and Phil Donahue into asking the candidates about it, Bill Clinton's student trip to Moscow became an issue even though Republicans spreading innuendo about it admitted they had no proof that Clinton had done anything wrong. The loosening of standards has accelerated since.[57]

The proliferation of New Media outlets also makes it harder for news organizations working on investigative stories to decide whether to run those stories on their own merits. When *Los Angeles Times* reporters Bill Rempel and Doug Frantz were working on the story about Arkansas state troopers who had allegedly helped arrange extramarital liaisons for then-governor Bill Clinton, Republican congressman Bob Dornan of California, guest-hosting the Rush Limbaugh program, announced that the paper was working on the story and was about to print it. "It makes it significantly harder to do your job," Rempel says, "when the sources from whom you are trying to get information are reacting to stories you haven't even printed yet."[58]

When Rempel was in Little Rock during the 1992 campaign tracking Clinton's background, Republican party sources began telling other news organizations that the *Los Angeles Times* was about to run a story about Clinton and drug use. Eventually, the Clinton campaign even felt compelled to deny the story in public, and the *Los Angeles Times* found itself in the curious position of printing a denial of a story it had never printed. In fact, the paper at the time was not even working on any such drug story.[59]

The problem may be even more acute in print than on television. With the luxury of space, newspapers can "bury" stories of this nature on their inside pages and argue that they have covered them without sensationalizing. And the record shows papers have been more inclined, indeed, to run such stories. On television, everything that airs appears, in effect, on the front page. And indeed the networks have proven more circumspect about running rumors.

Next, the national press, and television in particular, has reacted to the rise of New Media by suffering even greater pressure toward tabloidization. What do I mean by tabloidization? It is distinct from printing rumors or innuendo. Tabloidization has to do with news organizations devoting time and resources and prestige to covering subjects in proportion to public fascination rather than significance. It is entertainment and gossip rather than news. And while it is a part of all journalism, the percentage of time and space devoted to tabloid material has grown lately. ABC's Ted Koppel has likened good journalism to cartography. Like a map of a city, journalism reduces events in size and accessibility while remaining faithful to the basic features of the original. The metaphor suggests that journalism has a responsibility to proportion and context. And it implies need. It helps citizens make their way in a democratic, participatory republic. In this sense, tabloid or entertainment journalism is no more useful than the cartouches that decorated early charts and maps—intriguing, skillful, but generally placed in areas where the mapmakers didn't have real information.[60]

The mainstream press felt the pull of tabloidization during the 1992 campaign. When the Gennifer Flowers story broke, for instance, on the first night the networks resisted repeating the unsubstantiated allegations contained in the *Star* supermarket tabloid. But within twelve hours, after local affiliates and cable and the morning shows all played Flowers hard, the evening newscasts felt they no longer had any choice.

In 1994, in the wake of the stories involving Michael Jackson, the Menendez brothers' trial, and the Bobbitt trial, the trend has accelerated. "In many ways it feels like we are in a new era since the campaign," lamented NBC News vice president Bill Wheatley.[61]

Take the case of Tonya Harding. CBS's Connie Chung co-anchored the CBS "Evening News" for nearly two weeks from the skating rink in Oregon where Harding practiced. And this came at a time when the news in the Harding case could hardly be said to warrant such attention. During that entire period, the story had not materially changed: Harding's ex-husband had implicated her already, Harding continued to deny his allegations, and the police continued to investigate. Chung's executive producer, Erik Sorenson, even conceded that Chung was not there because the story warranted it. She was there because Chung was in Portland to woo Harding in the hopes that she would grant her first network interview to Chung's magazine program, "Eye to Eye." "And the only way to do that is to be there in person," Sorenson said, unless you offer to pay money, which the networks contend they won't do.[62] In effect, the tabloid-like network magazine shows had begun to shape the nature of the network evening newscasts. "The popularity of these syndicated news programs like 'Hard Copy' and the attention they pay to these ongoing soap operas have certainly bled all the way over into the rest of journalism," said Sorenson.

The tabloidization has occurred for two reasons. The first, as in the Gennifer Flowers case, is that the networks feel they must account in their broadcasts for what the public is learning from other sources. So if the *American Spectator* publishes a story full of innuendo, second-hand speculation, and reporter fancy about the love lives of the president and the first lady, which gets picked up on talk shows and eventually local news, the networks and other news organizations feel more pressure to air it. News organizations that decline to run a story that is gaining wide currency are criticized for sticking their heads in the sand. Even *New York Times* reporters criticized their own paper, for instance, for not covering the Gennifer Flowers story in 1992 more aggressively and to a lesser degree for not trying to cover the trooper sex story in January 1994.[63] In a sense, the media are losing their authority as the gatekeepers.

Now, some news organizations even use the widening spectrum of the media as an excuse *not* to exercise judgment. In the trooper story, for instance, CNN aired interviews with the troopers over the weekend after the *American Spectator* had begun to circulate, though it had time for only a scant effort to try to verify whether the troopers were telling the truth. ABC also did interviews with the troopers on Saturday afternoon, but did not air those stories until a few days later, after the story had circulated more widely.

The phenomenon of waiting to be second on a story is hardly new, but it has become a more convenient method of operation for journalists than before. At bottom, most of the electronic media are about conveying information, not gathering it. The requirements and expense of technology demand that. For much of the American media, increasingly so with the rise of New Media like talk radio, commenting on news actually gathered by others is their sole purpose.

The second reason for tabloidization is more complex. Prime-time network news magazines are proliferating because they are the surest and most efficient way to add to the news division's economic value. If one can launch a news magazine in prime time where previously an entertainment program was airing, the news division can create profit where there once was nothing. By contrast, trying to build the ratings of an existing nightly newscast that is going head to head against similar and entrenched competition is a difficult and uncertain process.

But once the news division competes in prime time against situation comedies and one-hour entertainment dramas, the pressure to make those shows as entertaining as possible grows enormously. Add to that the fact that these magazine programs often find themselves having to compete against syndicated tabloid shows like "Hard Copy" or "Inside Edition," which admit to paying money for news sources, especially when it comes to popular running stories like the Tonya Harding or Michael Jackson case.

At this point, it would be unfair to say that the tabloid nature of the magazine programs has meaningfully affected the coverage of the White House or even the governing process more generally. Nor are all the prime-time magazine shows tabloid-like in everything they do.

But there is reason to be concerned that the magazine shows are beginning to influence the rest of the news divisions. The first issue is that of crowding out: The time spent on tabloid stories is time not spent on anything except the most basic stories about the government and important public issues.

Beyond that, tabloidization will affect the hard news programs because of their importance to the networks and because of the effect they could have on public attitudes. Already, the work going into producing these programs gets amortized by finding its way into the evening news, as was the case with Chung co-anchoring from Portland. Eventually, the people who succeed in these programs may gain wider responsibility over the news. At ABC, for instance, the new executive producer of "World News Tonight with Peter Jennings," Rick Kaplan, came from "Prime Time Live," a show that, while it has done some serious work, made its name by using hidden cameras and owes more to the character of Diane Sawyer than political reporter Sam Donaldson. While Kaplan has fine hard-news credentials from before his work on "Prime Time Live," his magazine experience is influencing his work on the nightly news. After he joined "World News Tonight," for instance, the program hired a handwriting analyst to speculate about whether Tonya Harding had written the note found in a dumpster in Portland that may or may not have incriminated her in the crime. The story was remarkably similar to a piece on the tabloid program "American Journal," which even used the same handwriting analyst.

The pressures to fill the news with more tabloid stories is real. After a bruising internal battle over how to play the tabloid allegations of sex abuse made by Mia Farrow against Woody Allen in 1992, top executives at ABC News made producers on "World News Tonight" agree to incorporate more tabloid-type stories into the nightly news.

Paul Friedman, the executive producer of "World News" at the time, called them R&P stories, for rape and pillage.[64]

What is the effect, finally, on the public's relationship to the news divisions who produce these programs? The networks do not merely add these magazine shows to their schedule of news. They also invest their prestige in them. Increasingly, even the network anchors are working in the magazine shows: Dan Rather hosts "48 Hours," Tom Brokaw hosts "Now," and Jennings will be involved with "Turning Point." How will the public react the next time America goes to war and the press demands that the military allow it access to the battlefield in the name of the public interest? Who will the public believe the next time the press and the government clash over rights during a scandal or a national crisis, when the media charge they are working on behalf of the public's right to know and the government claims to be protecting national security? Can we expect the public to believe that the press has these lofty values at heart when it has given them so much tabloid journalism the rest of the time? And this is hardly restricted to the networks. The great newspapers were just as head over heels for Lorena Bobbitt and Tonya Harding and the Menendez brothers as anyone. A search on the Nexis news service reveals that the *New York Times, Washington Post,* and *Los Angeles Times* averaged more than two stories a day about the Harding affair for the month after Nancy Kerrigan was whacked on the knee. And one of those stories ran on page one every other day. Print journalism will also suffer a backlash.

The great risk of tabloidization, indeed, is its corrosion of public trust. The only truly valuable commodity that the press has is its credibility. If in the short term it compromises that, in the long term it will destroy itself.

Some journalists counter that today's economics require that the media indulge in tabloidization. The press must draw an audience to survive. The public likes these shows, after all, which is why the networks produce them. So how could producing popular programs destroy the networks' credibility?[65]

This economic argument, however, falters under a false view of audiences. People have different tastes for different situations. They may like to watch light entertainment in prime time. They might enjoy watching "Murphy Brown" and "Roseanne" for laughs, or Barbara Walters interviewing celebrities for gossip. But that does not mean people are happy if the great news organizations provide it, or devote a significant amount of their effort to it. As scholar Jay Rosen has argued, the great crisis facing the press, both television and print, is its loss of authority with the public.[66] We are losing our covenant with our audience. That, at heart, is why the 1992 presidential election was different from others. The public was repudiating the mainstream media's authority to mediate the campaign because of the way the media had operated and because of what they had become. In the nearly two years since the campaign ended, we in the media have adapted to that challenge by becoming at once more judgmental toward officials and at the same time more pandering to a public that we fear resents us. But we have not chosen the other alternative, to make the case for the "old" journalism—as distinguished from New Media—by holding more tightly to standards.

What are journalists to do then? How can a news organization resist, when the nation seems fixated on Lorena Bobbitt or Tonya Harding? How does one avoid the pack?

The real problem in the press is a failure of will. The most powerful journalists in the country have become fearful that if they impose standards, or say no to covering certain kinds of stories at the top of the news or on the front page and with generous space, then journalists will be accused of elitism. And elitism is part of what has left journalists out of touch.

This fear is misguided. It confuses the fact that we in the media have become isolated from the middle class by wealth, geography, and cultural ethos with the idea that we cannot then impose any personal or professional standards on the news. In fact, the opposite may be true. Most evidence suggests the public gravitates over time to journalists who demonstrate authentic qualities of professionalism, who consider journalism, as Humphrey Bogart described it in *Deadline USA*, as "the performance for public good," and who appeal to their audiences' higher nature. Consider that the highest-rated nightly newscasts over time have been those that were produced by the news divisions that demonstrated those qualities, first NBC's "Huntley–Brinkley Report," then CBS's with Walter Cronkite, and eventually ABC's with Peter Jennings. Consider that NBC has regained a solid number two rating in the nightly news in 1993 by returning to those qualities. Consider that a generation earlier, the survivors of the great newspaper wars—with exceptions—were the papers that similarly demonstrated those qualities: the *New York Times, Washington Post, Miami Herald, Philadelphia Inquirer, Los Angeles Times*. The survivors of this next revolution into new technology will also be those that demonstrate such public service, even at short-term cost. What the public requires from journalists has not changed because of technology. What the public requires from journalists, to the contrary, is even more crucial as the definition of media becomes broader.

9/BEYOND 1994

I f this is how Act Three of Ken Auletta's play has begun, how will it end?

For now, the media should be viewed as a spectrum of different points, which vary in significance depending on the circumstances. Most of the time, talk radio functions as an intercom for populist anger and alienation. Yet at moments when the political dialogue as expressed in the mainstream press becomes wildly out of sync with public sentiment, talk radio can become something more powerful. In January 1993, the mainstream press declared that it didn't matter much that attorney general-designate Zoe Baird had violated federal law in knowingly hiring illegal aliens and then also failing to pay Social Security taxes for them. A significant portion of the public disagreed, and talk radio provided it with a vehicle to register that complaint instantly. Once the Baird nomination had died, talk radio returned to its limited though important role.

"Larry King Live" on CNN has hardly supplanted the evening news, the morning newspapers, or the weekend network interview programs in communicating the discussion of politics in America. Yet when the Clinton administration decided it wanted to try to damage Ross Perot politically on the issue of the North American Free Trade Agreement by having Vice President Al Gore debate Perot, King's show was the perfect venue: It reached Perot supporters and was symbolically Perot's home court.

When the White House has wanted to target key congressional districts to lobby constituents for a specific member of Congress's vote, it arranged local satellite interviews. When the president felt he needed to demonstrate that he had nothing to hide on the Whitewater land deal, he held a prime-time televised press conference where he could face down the tough, noisy, traditional White House press corps. And when the president wanted to introduce major legislation on the budget or health care, he delivered addresses to joint sessions of Congress.

In part, this complex vision of the media spectrum reflects the changing and sophisticated way that the public—not just the president—uses the media. In the first moments of national and international crisis, for instance, the ratings for CNN surge, only to subside again within a few days. In moments of ongoing crisis, such as the Persian Gulf War or hurricanes, the network news ratings increase.

Town hall events become more important at moments when political leaders think that the mainstream press isn't letting them communicate directly and clearly with the people, as Clinton understood in March 1993 when the mainstream press was focused largely on his problems over gays in the military and he held a town hall meeting in Michigan. And entertainment and sports become important when politicians want to demonstrate that they are average folks or when they need to show they are undaunted by political controversy. So Bob Dole tries to change his nasty image by telling jokes on "The Tonight Show" with Jay Leno, and Al Gore tries to show he is not a political stiff by making fun of himself on David Letterman's "Late Night." Amid Whitewater, President Clinton sought to demonstrate that he is in touch with the average American by going to opening day of the baseball season in Cleveland and attending all the University of Arkansas games during the NCAA basketball championships.

In effect, choosing the right spot on the media spectrum has become part of the message. "When he went on MTV in the campaign," says presidential media adviser Mandy Grunwald, "what the president said was less important than that he was there, that he was reaching out to these young people."[67] He was communicating his ability and willingness to talk to them in their language, on their channel, and he was meeting them on their terms—and the other candidates weren't.

The key for the successful politician today is understanding the spectrum, and the public's changing and sophisticated use of it. The politician must also understand his own strengths and weaknesses. "Bill Clinton has an extraordinary ability to use these different mediums and not appear out of place," said Jeff Eller. "One of the things that will be interesting in 1994 and 1996 will be to watch people who think they can do these things learn they are not so easy. The other thing is these are no substitute for having something to say."[68]

Day in and day out, the mainstream press remains crucial for telling Americans the president's business. Thirty million households still tune into the three television networks, which in turn provide the basic footage and scripts for local news. It is a declining number, but still significant.

And nothing has replaced newspapers for filtering complex issues and setting much of the investigative and watchdog agenda. Roughly 25 percent of American homes still rely primarily on a daily newspaper, fewer than in the past, but still profound.

Yet at a given moment, talk radio or local television or cable may become more important. It depends on the audience, the message, and the situation.

Though its execution is often imperfect, the Clinton administration apparently understands this. But many journalists do not. Even as late as March 1994, ABC White House correspondent Ann Compton complained during a roundtable on television and the presidency that, "No president has done a better job of going around us, through us or behind our backs than has President Clinton." And CBS correspondent Randall Pinkston predicted that Clinton's efforts to bypass the press corps will "blow up in his face. There will come a time when he will regret not having the relationships with the Washington press corps that others have had."

Journalists must do a better job of understanding the New Media spectrum and their role in it. They need to realize that the fact the spectrum is widening does not mean their spot on it is disappearing. Only then will the mainstream press realize that it needs more than ever to maintain its traditional professional standards. If it looks longingly at the ratings of the tabloid shows, or the occasional influence of talk radio, it will be making a fatal mistake.

In effect, a larger part of the political dialogue now takes place outside the purview of journalists. What occurs beyond those journalistic boundaries, on talk radio or in direct satellite appearances, is also more open to distortion and innuendo than the political discourse the press conveys. That shift requires new responsibilities for journalists. The press needs to move further from being observers of the game to being the referee, for the game has surely become dirtier. The press needs to engage more often in pointing out distortions and demagoguery than it might have in the past, and do so in plain language. The movement toward publishing "truth boxes" to police political advertising is a step in the right direction. So is the movement to extend this referee role to the daily speeches of politicians. This is something that a few journalists did during the 1992 campaign. Larry Grossman, the former president of NBC News, has likened the emerging role of the mainstream press to that of firefighters, dedicated to putting out fires of false accusations and misunderstandings and maintaining the public well-being.[69]

This role of firefighter or referee needs to be properly understood. The press should be careful when trying to signify the meaning of events. Lippmann's admonition of seventy years ago still applies. When the press interprets, it should do so after having gathered the ideas of the institutional and intellectual forces of the community. For all of the accelerating pace of news and growing demand for context and analysis, journalists remain largely communicators, not analysts. Our skills are in gathering information and transmitting it to people's homes. We are masters of motion, not thought. We are skilled at gathering, even filtering, but not synthesizing. We are jacks of many trades, but rarely masters of any. And the quality of our instant analysis too often proves it. The public is not well served by soufflé journalism.

In the campaign of 1996, the New Media will regain a more important role than they have had in the interim since 1992, as the relationship between voters and politicians reaching out to them again becomes temporarily more direct and intense. The novelty of the New Media will also diminish somewhat. Bill Clinton will not distinguish himself just because he did town halls and Arsenio Hall's show and George Bush didn't. Every Republican will do New Media, if only to avoid Bush's mistake. This will reduce the significance of the appearances, and raise the significance of what the candidates actually say.

As this change occurs, the press should do the following:

▲   Understand the role of the New Media better and not be so frightened of it.

▲   Show more courage in maintaining standards than it has so far in order to distinguish it from the New Media. Specifically, the leaders of the great networks and newspapers should initiate a public debate over standards to help the public understand these issues.

▲   Play the role of referee over the public dialogue, much of which is carried out through the New Media, without overplaying its hand as pundit. To do so, publish more truth boxes that scrutinize political advertising and political rhetoric generally, and be more systematic about it than in 1992. The public will respond and respect the effort.

▲ Use polls and reporting more to discern what voters' major concerns are about their own lives and focus their coverage around those concerns. And use polls less to gauge the president's popularity as the main lens of politics.

▲ Strive to change the focus of coverage from who is winning to what information about candidates would help voters decide who to support. To do so, the press should use computer technology now available to do some simple content analysis of its own work, making sure that it is keeping the nature of its coverage well mixed.

▲ Write background pieces about candidates in ways that are less often investigative exposes and more often strike the tone of features. During campaigns, the pace of events and the difficulty of trying to capture the totality of a candidate's life make the expose model often an inadequate and unfair approach to exploring a candidate's background.

▲ As often as possible, scrutinize candidates' background and prepare these profiles before the primary season is well under way. Once the primaries are off and running, doing serious stories examining a candidate's background becomes much more difficult.

▲ After the election, redouble efforts, again, to focus on governing and policy by doing fewer stories on how the president is doing and more on what he is doing.

▲ Finally, I suggest the press embark on a radical but mature approach to covering the private lives of candidates. Announce in advance that the traditional press is going to explore such areas as personal morality and personal background more intensely, including asking candidates whether they have committed adultery. Only by doing this can the mainstream press

avoid leaving the job to the sensational and unfair standards of
the tabloid press, which will have no compunctions about it.

Let me explain. Those who object to the press's coverage of candidates' sex lives argue, among other things, that we are unfairly driv-
ing good people from public office. Committing adultery does not necessarily mean someone cannot be a good president, but the press has
set up a standard where they might not be elected, or might not even
subject themselves to running. The press, these critics argue, should
return to the old standard of not publishing the details of someone's
private lives unless or until it can be proven relevant to one's public
conduct. Hence Wayne Hays's affair with Elizabeth Ray was news only
when it was discovered she was on the public payroll.

The problem with this argument, however much merit it might
have, is that it is no longer possible to sustain it and even betrays
naivete about the New Media universe. Today, as we have seen above,
if the mainstream press ignores a candidate's private life, the stories
will eventually make their way into the campaign anyway through the
New Media, usually in the most sensational terms, and the mainstream
press will find itself covering it on the worst possible terms. The press,
as we have seen, simply no longer has the power of gatekeeper.

The only solution is for the press to play the role of firefighter.
And the only way to handle this kind of fire is to create what in effect is
a fire break, setting controlled fires that scorch the earth to keep the
wildfire from spreading.

To keep the tabloids from running out of control, in other words,
the mainstream press today must publish the material about candidates' private lives in advance, in a responsible way, and allow the public to decide its relevance for itself. In 1992 the public already demonstrated it could do that more maturely than it had been given credit for.

The approach would work as follows. The press would put all
presidential candidates on notice that they would be asked as a matter
of course about adultery, drugs, medical records, and other issues that
might potentially provoke the tabloids. More than that, the mainstream press would aggressively investigate these issues, to put a
penalty on candidates' lying. The press would explain that it was doing
this precisely because the tabloids were going to pursue these issues,
so that the best way to handle them responsibly was to do so in
advance, voluntarily, in the mainstream press, and allow the public
to decide.

Currently, the press covers these matters like adolescents sneaking into R-rated movies. It is not sure whether it thinks it matters, so we skirt around the issue, making occasional forays into reporting about personal conduct, but only sporadically, and usually larding up the stories with torturously elaborate justifications about why we are doing so. Or worse, we gather the information but then wait for more sensational journals to break the story.

The approach I am advocating would end this. In effect, it would take the issue of relevance out of the newsroom and put it in the public sector. And by so doing, it would take back the agenda from the tabloid or ideologically motivated press. Part of what gives the tabloids and the party journals their power is the fear and sense of continuing taboo felt by the mainstream press. Eliminate the taboo, and we reduce the power of the tabloids. If candidates had already broached the subject themselves in the *New York Times* or *Washington Post*, voluntarily, they would be largely inoculated from further damage if they had been open and honest in their account. And if the tabloids came out with information that was false or distorted, the mainstream press would be in a position to say so authoritatively, the firefighter role in the best sense.

In addition to defusing the tabloids, the approach has two other virtues. It would allow the candidates to come forward honestly rather than be put on the defensive in the middle of a campaign. And by bringing the issue out in the open, this approach might set the issue of adultery and other personal matters in a proper context, so that adultery, per se, might not disqualify otherwise deserving candidates from public office, if the public so deems it.

If properly handled, the press in effect would be catching up to a culture that has already moved ahead of our worn sense of protecting people from information, and probably helping the culture come to grips with an issue that is now a recurring and significant matter of public debate.

Taken together, these recommendations amount to a plea that we in the press referee campaigns on behalf of voters as they play out through a broader media spectrum. Do not limit the press's role to simply calling the race. And do not be afraid of being journalists. If what we write and publish is important, the public will respond.

NOTES

1. Kathleen Hall Jamieson, "The Subversive Effects of a Focus on Strategy in News Coverage of Presidential Campaigns," in *1-800-PRESIDENT: The Report of the Twentieth Century Fund Task Force on Television and the Campaign of 1992* (New York: The Twentieth Century Fund Press, 1993).

2. Ken Auletta, "On and Off the Bus: Lessons from Campaign '92," in *1-800-PRESIDENT*.

3. Ibid.

4. Thomas E. Patterson, "Let the Press Be the Press," in *1-800-PRESIDENT*.

5. Sidney Blumenthal, "A Letter From Washington," *The New Yorker*, April 5, 1993.

6. Ibid.

7. Ibid.

8. Statistics prepared by the White House.

9. Ibid.

10. The author heard or saw compact disks of these groups in the offices of White House staff working in the Old Executive Office Building during interviews in March 1993.

11. Broder told this joke himself in a speech he delivered to the American Society of Newspaper Editors Convention in Baltimore in April 1993.

12. Interview with White House correspondent from Reuters, March 1993.

13. Strauss showed the radio equipment to the author during a tour of the facilities, March 1993.

14. Interview with Strauss, October 1992, first cited by author in *Strange Bedfellows: How Television and the Presidential Candidates Changed American Politics*, 1992 (Westport, Conn.: Hyperion Press, July 1993).

15. Interviews with Eller, Anderson, and Strauss, March and April 1993.

16. Interview with Stephanopoulos, March 1993.

17. Several reporters recounted this or events like it happening to them in interviews with Stephanopoulos. So did others who worked with Stephanopoulos. The quotes cited here were said by Stephanopoulos's secretary in the presence of the author during his interview with Stephanopoulos.

18. Interview with a senior White House official, June 1993.

19. Interview with Hume by author, March 1993.

20. Interview with Deaver, March 1993.

21. Interview with Gergen, then editor-at-large of *U.S. News & World Report*, March 1993.

22. Interviews with Deaver, Stephanopoulos, Myers, and Deputy Communications Director Ricki Seidman, March 1993.

23. Interviews with two high-ranking campaign advisers to Clinton who did not work in the White House under Stephanopoulos, March 1993.

24. Interview with Lauter, April 1993.

25. Interview with Tutwiler, January 1994.

26. "Nightline," May 21, 1993.

27. Hunt said this on several programs during the week, including the "Today Show" and CNN's "Capitol Gang," and repeated it in an interview, June 1993.

28. Interview with Anderson, March 1993.

29. Interview with Eller, March 1993.

30. Interview with Stephanopoulos, March 1993.

31. These figures are based on a private White House document supplied to the author that lists every television interview President Clinton conducted with local media around the country.

32. Statistics prepared by the White House.

33. Interview with Duffy, December 1993.

34. White House local television document.

35. White House local television document.

36. Interviews with Eller and Anderson, March and April 1993. The author also watched these video press conferences as they were occurring from the White House television studio in Room 456 of the Old Executive Office Building.

37. Interviews with Eller and Anderson, March 1993.

38. Interview with Eller, March 1993.

39. Interview with Eller and Anderson, March 1993.
40. Interviews with Eller and Anderson, March 1993.
41. Interviews with Eller and Anderson, March 1993.
42. Interviews with more than a dozen White House reporters, September and October 1993.
43. Interview with White House Communications Director Mark Gearan, October 1993, plus White House reporter interviews.
44. Interviews with White House reporters, March 1993.
45. Ibid.
46. Interview with Gearan, August 1993.
47. The Center for Media and Public Affairs is a nonprofit, nonpartisan research organization. The results of their analysis are available from the center's office in Washington.
48. The public opinion surveys cited here compare the public's approval ratings of Bill Clinton's job performance from *Washington Post*-ABC, CBS-*New York Times*, Gallup CNN-*USA Today*, the *Los Angeles Times*, and also the Times Mirror Center for People and the Press.
49. This sentiment is clear from dozens of interviews the author had conducted over several years with journalists covering politics.
50. Several sources have described this moment in particular and others like it as meaningful and illustrative. ABC "World News Tonight" executive producer Paul Friedman cited the Donahue appearance as a turning point in interviews with the author for *Strange Bedfellows*. Jamieson, *1-800-PRESIDENT*, also cited it.
51. Interview with Jennings, May 1992, cited in *Strange Bedfellows*.
52. In *1-800-PRESIDENT*, Jamieson praises the ad-policing the press conducted, though the author details in *Strange Bedfellows* how this ad-policing was more sporadic and open to manipulation by candidates than it should have been.
53. This analysis is based on a study the author conducted with the help of the Center for Media and Public Affairs. For this paper, the author studied a randomly selected cross section of 25 percent of all the stories to appear on the nightly newscasts of the three major broadcast networks, ABC, CBS, and NBC.
54. The author conducted this content analysis of the front pages of the *Los Angeles Times*, *New York Times*, and *Washington Post* over two months in the spring of 1993 for a project conducted for the *Los Angeles Times*.
55. Interview with Broder, August 1993.

56. Interview with Brownstein, August 1993.

57. The material was printed in a financial newsletter produced by Johnson Smick International, Inc., a Washington consulting firm headed by two people connected to Republican politicians.

58. Interview with Rempel, March 1994.

59. "Clinton Tells of Marijuana Use in '60s," *Los Angeles Times*, March 30, 1992. Interview with Rempel, March 1994.

60. Ted Koppel, "The Worst Is Yet to Come," *Washington Post*, April 3, 1994.

61. Conversation with Wheatley, March 1994.

62. Interview with Erik Sorenson, executive producer of "The CBS Evening News with Dan Rather," January 1994.

63. See Rosenstiel, *Strange Bedfellows*, about the criticism the *New York Times* suffered for downplaying the Gennifer Flowers story in January 1992.

64. See Rosenstiel, *Strange Bedfellows*, p. 244

65. This is precisely the argument Phil Donahue made to defend the change that came over his program in the late 1980s in response to the rise of Oprah Winfrey and Geraldo Rivera. See the transcripts of a panel Donahue was on at the American Society of Newspaper Editors convention in Washington, D.C., April 12, 1989, entitled "Who's a Journalist: Talk Show Sensationalism," about the rise of daytime talk shows.

66. Interviews with Jay Rosen, New York University. See also Jay Rosen's essay, "Politics, Vision, and the Press: Toward a Public Agenda for Journalism," in *The New News v. The Old News* (New York: The Twentieth Century Fund Press, 1992).

67. Interview with Grunwald, August 1993.

68. Interview with Eller, April 1994.

69. Larry Grossman made this argument at a panel attended by the author in March 1994 at the Joan Shorenstein Barone Center at Harvard University sponsored by the Markle Foundation.

INDEX

ABC (American Broadcasting
  Corporation), 24, 26, 32, 33,
  38, 39, 41
"American Journal" (TV pro-
  gram), 39
American Spectator, 38
Anderson, David, 8, 12, 15
Arizona, 16
Arizona Republic, 16
"Arsenio Hall" (TV program), 7
Aspin, Les, 20
Auletta, Ken, 5, 43

Baird, Zoe, 43
Blumenthal, Sidney, 7
Bogart, Humphrey, 41
Broder, David, 8–9
Broder, John M., 31
Brownstein, Ronald, 32–33
Budget: Clinton's, 16, 21, 31; for
  communications, 16
Bush, George, 9; relations with
  media, 10, 14, 21

California, 16, 17
Call-in format (New Media), 23
Candidates and media, 47, 48, 49
Carter, Jimmy: relations with
  media, 14

CBS (Columbia Broadcasting
  System), 2, 41
"CBS Evening News" (TV pro-
  gram), 24, 37
Center for the Media and Public
  Affairs, 21
Charlotte (N.C.), 17
Charlotte Observer, 24
Chung, Connie, 37, 39
Clinton, Bill: coverage in media
  of, 17, 22, 31, 36, 39, 47;
  image in media of, 2, 11–12, 21,
  28, 31–32; relations with
  media, 1, 8, 9, 11, 14–15, 20,
  44, 46
Clinton, Hillary Rodham, 8, 14
Clinton administration, 8–9,
  11, 12; relations with media, 7,
  22, 43–44, 45
CNN (Cable News Network), 13,
  17–18, 21, 44
Compton, Ann, 45
Content analysis, 21–22, 30
C-SPAN (TV channel), 12, 36

Deaver, Michael, 10
Democrats, 9, 11
Dole, Bob, 44
Dornan, Bob, 36

Dowd, Maureen, 33
Duffy, Michael, 14

Electorate. See Voters
Eller, Jeff, 9, 16, 18, 44
Events: coverage of, 11, 12, 26–28

Flowers, Gennifer, 37, 38
Ford, Gerald: relations with
  media, 14
Foster, Vince, 22, 35
Frantz, Doug, 36
Friedman, Paul, 40, 52 n50

Gays in the military, 17, 20–21,
  28, 44
Generation gap, 8–9, 11
Gergen, David, 10, 19, 20
Gibble, Ernie, 8
Gore, Al, 14, 43, 44
Greenfield, Jeff, 32
Grossman, Larry, 46
Grunwald, Mandy, 44

Haircut story, 11, 12, 17
Harding, Tonya, 37, 39
Hays, Wayne, 48
Health care reform, 16, 17, 21
Hopper, Kim, 8
Horse race reporting, 4, 5, 23, 24,
  26–28
Hubbell, Webster, 22
Hume, Brit, 10
Hunt, Al, 12

Interpretive reporting, 30–33
Interviews: by Clinton administration, 8, 12, 14, 15, 43
Issues, 23; coverage of, 5, 16, 17,
  20–22, 26, 28

Jamieson, Kathleen Hall, 4, 5, 52
  n52
Jennings, Peter, 24, 39
Journalists, 24, 29; attitudes of,
  5, 8–9, 11, 23, 41, 46; com-
  plaints by, 8, 10, 45; judgments
  by, 31, 32–33. See also Old
  Media; White House press
  corps

Kaplan, Rick, 39
Koppel, Ted, 12, 37

"Larry King Live" (TV program),
  5, 17, 23, 36, 43
"Late Night" (TV program), 44
Lauter, David, 11
Lippmann, Walter, 5, 46
Limbaugh, Rush, 35, 36
Local media, 12, 16, 17–18, 29,
  34, 45
Los Angeles Times, 21, 30, 31, 36
Louisiana, 16

Mainstream press, 12, 31, 45;
  and Clinton administration,
  44; and 1992 campaign, 23–24,
  37; role of, 46, 47–48, 49
Media, 16; control by, 1, 18, 38;
  manipulation of, 27; relations
  with the public, 2, 12–13, 23,
  24, 28, 33–34, 40–41, 46, 47;
  role of, 17, 45
Miami (Fla.), 17
Moynihan, Daniel Patrick, 35
Myers, Dee Dee, 10, 19. See also
  New Media; Old Media
Myths: about Clinton
  administration, 2, 7, 8, 9–10,
  13, 15; about media, 18

National media, 12–13, 16; and
Clinton administration, 10–11,
14, 17
NBC (National Broadcasting
Corporation), 41
Networks. *See* Television net-
works
Nevada, 16
New Media, 3, 7, 36, 48; influ-
ence of, 23, 38; role of, 2, 18, 46;
use by Clinton administration,
2, 9, 10, 12, 13, 16, 43–44
News conferences. *See* Press
conferences
Newspapers, 30-31, 36, 41–42, 45
See also specific newspapers,
e.g., *Washington Post*
New York Times, 2, 21, 30, 32, 33,
38
"Nightline" (TV program), 12
Nixon, Richard: relations with
media, 14

Objectivity in reporting: lack of,
3, 25, 30–33
Old Executive Office Building, 9, 15
Old Media, 1; coverage of politics by, 4–5, 27, 31–32, 35–36,
38; changes in, 3, 18, 22, 24–25,
29, 39–40; economics of, 38,
39, 40; obsolescence of, 2, 7, 8,
23, 38; role of, 3, 5, 37, 41, 42,
45–48, 49
1-800-PRESIDENT, 4, 5

Patterson, Thomas E., 5
Perot, Ross, 1, 5, 43
"Phil Donahue Show" (TV pro-
gram), 23, 36, 53 n65
Pinkston, Randall, 45

Political communication, 3, 7,
43–44, 45–46; in 1992 campaign, 1–2, 9
Political leadership and the
media, 2, 4, 7, 10
Politicians: and the media, 27, 44,
45–46; sexual liaisons of, 21,
36, 37, 38, 48, 49; and voters, 3,
5, 17, 23, 46, 48
Politics: coverage of, 4–5, 26,
28–29, 31–32, 43; vs. governance, 26, 27, 47
Presidential campaign (1992), 1, 23;
coverage of, 4, 5, 18, 24, 28, 36,
37, 46
Presidential campaign (1996):
role of media in, 46–49
Press. *See* Journalists; Old Media;
White House press corps
Press conferences, 8, 14, 15–17,
43–44
Primaries, 1, 5, 28, 47
"Prime Time Live" (TV program), 39
Public opinion, 39; changes in, 1;
and Clinton administration,
21, 22, 26
Public service role of media, 3,
41, 42, 48

Radio, 9, 35
Radio talk shows, 16–17, 34, 43,
45
Rather, Dan, 32
Reagan, Ronald: relations with
media, 8, 14, 21
Reagan administration: relations
with media, 11, 13
Rempel, Bill, 36
Reporters. *See* Journalists
Republican party, 9, 18, 36, 46

Risen, James, 31
Rosen, Jay, 41

Sarmiento, Jess, 8
Sensationalism in coverage, 4, 48
Sorenson, Erik, 37
Standards: journalistic, 3, 25,
    35–41, 45, 46, 48
Stephanopoulos, George, 8–11,
    12, 19
Strauss, Richard, 8, 9
Subjectivity in reporting, 25,
    30–33
Sun City Daily News, 16

Tabloid press, 25, 36–40, 45, 48,
    49
Talks shows, 12, 24, 34, 35, 43, 45;
    and Clinton administration,
    16–17; and 1992 campaign, 5,
    7, 23
Technology and politics, 5, 15,
    18, 30–31, 47
Television, 2, 36, 38–39; and
    Clinton administration, 8,
    15–18, 26; economics of, 38, 39;
    and 1992 campaign, 24, 37
Television audiences, 12–13, 34,
    45
Television networks, 17–18, 21,
    33–34, 36, 37–38, 41
Thematic approach to news,
    28–29

Time: influence on media, 27, 32;
    limits on, 16
Time (magazine), 31–32
"Tonight Show" (TV program), 44
Travel by Clinton, 21; coverage
    of, 11, 17, 44
Travel office story, 12, 17
Tutwiler, Margaret, 11

Upper Press Office, 11

Voters: access to politicians by,
    3, 23, 43, 46; and the media, 2;
    and 1992 campaign, 5, 24

Wall Street Journal, 32
Washington Post, 26, 30, 35
White House Communications
    Department, 9–10, 18
White House press corps, 33;
    relations with Clinton admin-
    istration, 2, 7, 8–11, 14–15,
    19–20, 43, 45
White House staff, 8; criticism of,
    8–9, 11, 12
Whitewater story, 17, 21–22, 35,
    43–44
Wisconsin, 16
Wooten, Jim, 24
"World News Tonight" (TV pro-
    gram), 24, 39–40

ABOUT THE AUTHOR

Tom Rosenstiel is Washington media and political correspondent for the *Los Angeles Times*. He is the author of *Strange Bedfellows: How Television and the Presidential Candidates Changed American Politics, 1992* and for the past six years has made a specialty of studying how the press and technology influence political events. In 1991, he won the Lowell Mellett Award for Outstanding Media Criticism for his coverage of the role of technology in the opening of Eastern Europe, the changing nature of television news, and the role of the media in the buildup of the Gulf War. Prior to joining the *Los Angeles Times*, he was at the *Peninsula Times Tribune* in Palo Alto, California, and also worked for Jack Anderson's column, "Washington Merry Go Round."

PERSPECTIVES

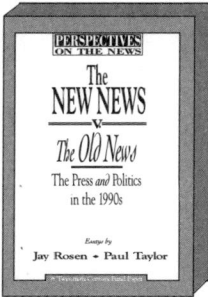

*T*wo years ago, the Twentieth Century Fund began a project to examine—and improve—the performance of the press. Our Perspectives on the News series features important journalists and academics exploring current press issues and offering recommendations for change. Each in the series is a valuable tool for journalists and anyone else who cares about the role the press plays in making sure we have an informed democracy which, after all, is the only kind of democracy that can survive.

ESSAYS BY JAY ROSEN AND PAUL TAYLOR

Jay Rosen is associate professor of journalism at New York University and a former journalist.

Paul Taylor is a reporter for the Washington Post.

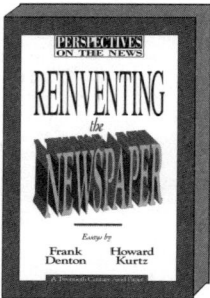

THE NEW NEWS V. THE OLD NEWS
THE PRESS AND POLITICS IN THE 1990S

*T*he two essays in this volume explore the changes and growing pressures arising from talk shows, call-in radio, and other challenges to the existing press order. "Politics, Vision, and the Press: Toward a Public Agenda for Journalism," by Jay Rosen; "Political Coverage in the 1990s: Teaching the Old News New Tricks," by Paul Taylor.

75 PAGES, 0–87078–344–0, $9.95

REINVENTING THE NEWSPAPER

*A*re newspapers still relevant in the age of instantaneous television news coverage? In "Old Newspapers and New Realities: The Promise of the Marketing of Journalism," Frank Denton argues that newspapers must reinvent themselves to compete and survive in the free market. In "Yesterday's News: Why Newspapers Are Losing Their Franchise," Howard Kurtz traces the history of newspapers and offers prescriptions for how newspapers can regain their edge in an era dominated by television.

119 PAGES, 0–87078–350–5, $9.95

ESSAYS BY FRANK DENTON AND HOWARD KURTZ

Frank Denton is editor of the Wisconsin State Journal.

Howard Kurtz is a reporter for the Washington Post.

ON THE NEWS

COVERING THE WORLD
INTERNATIONAL TELEVISION NEWS SERVICES

*L*ewis A. Friedland examines the impact of CNN and other international television news services on traditional network news departments and on the events themselves. Friedland shows how the global coverage of events as they occur—in "real time"— complicates the governing of nations.

61 PAGES, 0–87078–345–9, $8.95

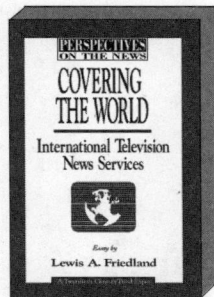

LEWIS A. FRIEDLAND

is assistant professor in the School of Journalism and Mass Communication at the University of Wisconsin-Madison and a producer with Wisconsin Public Television.

AT WHAT PRICE?
LIBEL LAW AND FREEDOM OF THE PRESS

*T*his book investigates the effects of libel litigation and punitive damages on a free press. In "The 'Muzzled Media': Constitutional Crisis or Product Liability Scam?" Martin London examines the dangerous aspects of media corporations that pursue profit while operating under First Amendment protection. In "Libel Law Doesn't Work, but Can It Be Fixed?" Barbara Dill looks at libel litigation as well as recent efforts to reform the process.

79 PAGES, 0–87078–356–4, $9.95

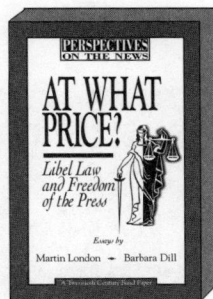

ESSAYS BY
MARTIN LONDON
AND BARBARA DILL

Martin London is a partner in the law firm of Paul, Weiss, Rifkind, Wharton & Garrison.

Barbara Dill is a lawyer specializing in seminars for journalists on how to prevent libel and privacy suits.

TO ORDER CALL: 1–800–275–1447

TASK FORCE REPORTS

1–800–PRESIDENT

THE REPORT OF THE TWENTIETH CENTURY FUND TASK FORCE ON TELEVISION AND THE CAMPAIGN OF 1992

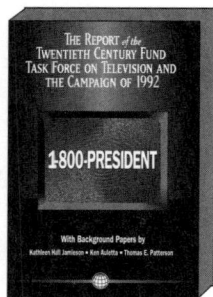

*H*ow is television spinning presidential campaigns? Early in 1992, the Twentieth Century Fund brought together a group of prominent individuals from the press, politics, academia, and the financial and foundation communities to examine television's influence on the presidential election. The Task Force was chaired by Ben Bradlee, vice president at large of the *Washington Post*, and included, among others, network anchors Peter Jennings and Tom Brokaw, and Twentieth Century Fund Board members Theodore C. Sorensen and Congressman James A. Leach.

134 PAGES, 0–87078–349–1, $9.95

Background papers by Kathleen Hall Jamieson, Ken Auletta, and Thomas E. Patterson

QUALITY TIME?

THE REPORT OF THE TWENTIETH CENTURY FUND TASK FORCE ON PUBLIC TELEVISION

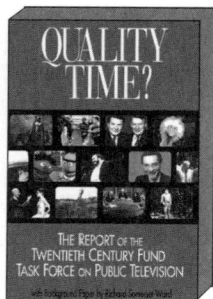

*T*wenty-five years after its founding, public television in America faces an array of challenges. In this Task Force Report, which precipitated a flurry of articles and editorials and continues to generate public discussion, a group of prominent individuals from the media, foundation, and public policy communities offers sharp and substantive recommendations for improving the nation's public television system. The Task Force, which was chaired by Brown University president Vartan Gregorian, concluded that there is a more pressing need than ever for an alternative to the market-driven programming offered by commercial stations and cable systems.

200 PAGES, 0–87078–177–4, $9.95

Background paper by Richard Somerset-Ward.

TO ORDER CALL: 1–800–275–1447